Waiting and Longing

Being *Ready* for the Return of Jesus, *Whenever* It Happens

RANDALL L. ROBERTS

PACIFIC PRESS® PUBLISHING ASSOCIATION

Nampa, Idaho

Oshawa, Ontario, Canada

www.PacificPress.com

Inside design by Aaron Troia
Cover photo provided by the author
Cover design by Gerald Lee Monks

Additional copies of this book are available by calling toll-free
1-800-765-6955 or visiting http://www.adventistbookcenter.com

Library of Congress Cataloging-in-Publication Data:

Roberts, Randall L., 1959-
Waiting and longing : being ready for the return of Jesus
whenever it happens / Randall L. Roberts.
p.cm.
ISBN 13: 978-0-8163-2534-4
ISBN 10: 0-8163-2534-0
1. End of the world. 2. Second Advent. I.Title: End is near. II. Title.

BT877.R63 2003

236'.9—dc21   2002044958

11 12 13 14 • 5 4 3 2

Dedication

To Mom and Dad,
who love the Word
and live the Word.

Acknowledgments

I have discovered that writing a book is both a lonely and a communal task. It is lonely because of the many hours spent in solitude, playing with words and concepts, trying to make the right words express the correct concepts. But it is never *only* a lonely task. Even what happens in solitude is influenced and formed by what happens in community. A large and beloved community of former teachers, pastors, colleagues, and friends has influenced me in the direction of what appears in these pages. They are too numerous to name here, but their imprint on my life is forever appreciated.

There are several, however, who must be named.

As stated in the Preface, Dr. Jon Paulien was the first to point out the context of the parables herein studied. I express my gratitude to him.

It is highly questionable if this book would ever have been written had it not been for Intissar Issa. Intissar has been an overly patient source of encouragement and work. She has prodded me when I was tempted to give up, has spent hours poring over the manuscript, smoothing out the rough edges of my writing, and has made invaluable suggestions that contribute to the final product. God bless you, Intissar, for your hard work, your kind spirit, and your passion for seeing the message in print!

Jack Brown, a faithful friend and expert research collaborator, has spent hours tracking down details, stories, and other necessary information. Thank you, Jack!

Finally, the three dearest people in my life have been extremely patient with long hours of time in the study. Miranda, thank you for your hugs and kisses! Austin, now we'll have a little more time for basketball! And to my wife and best friend, Anita, thank you for being my partner, friend, and companion as we journey with Jesus. You are God's gift to me!

Contents

What Do We Watch?

This is a book about watching for the second coming of Christ. Specifically, it is a book about *how to watch* for the return of Christ. Matthew 24 (and the parallel passages of Mark 13 and Luke 21) describe the day when Jesus left the temple grounds for the last time and His disciples came to Him and pointed out the grandeur and splendor of the temple. His response must have stunned them. " 'Do you see all these things?' he asked. 'Truly I tell you, not one stone here will be left on another; every one will be thrown down' " (Matthew 24:2, TNIV). They couldn't conceive of such a thing! So later, as He sat on the Mount of Olives, they came to Him with the question, "Tell us, . . . when will this happen, and what will be the sign of your coming and of the end of the age?" (verse 3, TNIV). In answering their question, Jesus begins by saying, "Watch out . . ." (verse 4, TNIV). In other words, "Take care! Be careful!" Clearly, in preparation for such a cataclysmic event, He urged His followers toward watchfulness and preparation.

Sobering, isn't it? Little wonder that, throughout time, the followers of Jesus have placed such a decided emphasis on watching for His return. Yet, an understandable question arises, What does it mean to watch? Where do we focus our attention? *What exactly do we watch?* If nothing else, church history has taught us that Christians have watched a variety of different realities as ways to prepare for the coming of Christ.

Many have watched the turbulent, deadly events in nature. After all, in the first part of His answer to the disciples' question, Jesus gives a list of signs of His coming. Included among those signs are events in nature. "There will be famines and earthquakes in various places" (verse 7b, TNIV).

Earthquakes, floods, tornadoes, hurricanes, and a tragically long list of other natural disasters have been the focus of attention for many. Thus, when yet another storm unleashes its fury upon us, many say, "It's just one more sign of the nearness of Christ's coming." And since such events seem to happen with increased frequency and intensity, surely they signify an imminent end. So some think, *If we can just keep their symbolism on our radar screens, watching these events will help us to be ready for the end they portend.*

Others watch the political and international news. After all, when giving the signs of the end, Jesus *also* said, "You will hear of wars and rumors of wars. . . . Nation will rise against nation, and kingdom against kingdom" (verses 6, 7, TNIV). So we ought to keep a very close eye on international conflict, crisis, and instability. A keen awareness of what happens on that front will help us to be ready.

Along these same lines, many of Christ's followers have kept an eye on religious and political leaders around the globe. What are world leaders doing? Is the president of the United States making choices and helping to enact legislation that jeopardizes religious liberty? What about the pope? Is he gaining in strength and prestige? Are leaders in the United Nations and other countries hindering the progress of the gospel and opposing or, on the other hand, contributing to religious intolerance and persecution? There has been a tendency to view all such events through the prism of the last day drama.

Others have watched the state of the Christian church. "It must be close to the end. After all, isn't the church in a Laodicean condition? And didn't Jesus say that 'the love of most will grow cold'?" (verse 12, TNIV). In the same vein, some have constructed elaborate charts that detail the events that will unfold at the end, and have become so familiar with these as to imply that salvation will come through a thorough knowledge of such charts. So they keep an eye on the charts and the news! And some Christians have even said that what we need is to be watchful by working for a generation of perfect (read *sinless*) Christians, as the last generation before His coming (they say) will be a perfect one.

This is not an exhaustive list of the realities that Christians have watched with reference to the coming of Christ. It may, however, suffice to underline that there are many different issues upon which Christians throughout time have focused their attention—many different things we have *watched* in our attempt to be ready for His coming.

Here, however, is what is of *great* interest: none of these—*none of these*—is what Jesus tells us to watch. While some of these matters may play roles in the final denouement of earth's history, they are not the issues that are central to Him (in Matthew 24 and 25) in terms of watching for His coming. The truth is, in the context of His final discourse in Matthew, He is very specific about what it means to watch for His coming.

As if to underline the importance of what He says in these two chapters of Matthew, consider a statement recorded in Mark's Gospel from the same incident (see Mark 13). Mark's is a much more abbreviated version of this event, particularly when it comes to the parables that Jesus tells. But there is one line that is particularly noteworthy. It appears right at the end of the incident and is thus the last line of this section. It is the take-home lesson that Jesus gives His disciples. It's almost as though He says, "Now, in light of everything I have said about My coming, about its certainty, about the signs that lead up to it, and about the necessity of always being ready for it, here is the last thing I have to say."

Well, with a lead-in like that, we want to know—*What is the take-home lesson, Jesus?* And He doesn't disappoint us, for here is what He says, "What I say to you, I say to everyone, 'Watch!' " (Mark 13:37, TNIV).

Watch. *Watch!* That has an ominous ring to it, doesn't it? *Stay alert! Pay attention! Keep awake!* If you're anything like me, there is an obvious question that follows: *How? How* am I to watch? What does it mean to watch?

Such is the theme of this book.

Three notes are in order.

First, we certainly ought not to think that other biblical passages dealing with the coming of Christ are secondary. Daniel and Revelation and parts of 2 Thessalonians (to name a few) are of equally valid importance. But none is as succinct and straightforward regarding *what it means to watch* for the coming of Christ as Jesus is here in Matthew's Gospel.

Second, every so often, another hysteria erupts regarding the end of the world and the coming of Christ. A movement emerges, a religious leader speaks, sometimes a date is set, and everyone's attention is galvanized once again on the theme. Many laugh and taunt the news while others believe it. But some straddle the fence, outwardly denying they believe it and stating they have no concern about it, but inwardly wondering, *If it did happen, would I be ready? Have I done what I need to do in terms of watching so that I can face His coming with a quiet assurance that I will meet Him in peace?* Jesus helps us answer such questions.

And third, it must be underlined and stated time and again: whether the coming of Jesus happens *just around the corner* or whether it happens a thousand years from now, one central reality never changes—*we are saved by Jesus and His righteousness.* The Bible does *not* teach salvation by knowledge. Nor does it teach salvation by charts. Nor does it teach salvation by following the news or by watching the president or the pope or by becoming perfect or by knowing exactly *what* will happen *when* or by any method other than receiving salvation as the free gift that Jesus, by His grace, offers us. The Bible teaches salvation by faith in Jesus Christ. *Period.*

Yet, even those who walk with Jesus in a saving relationship need to hear what He says regarding watching for His coming. After all, it was to His disciples that He said, "So you also must be ready, because the Son of Man will come at an hour when you do not expect him" (Matthew 24:44, TNIV).

It is to that end that I offer the re-publication of this book.

Randy Roberts
Senior Pastor
Loma Linda University Church

CHAPTER ONE

The Certainty

I grew up certain that I *wouldn't* grow up—Jesus was coming too soon! That reality dominated many aspects of my Christian childhood. I was certain that I would not attend college, would not marry and have children, would not enter professional life, and would not own a home. I was certain that I would not do any of the things that we normally associate with growing up. Jesus would return in the clouds of heaven to take home the redeemed before any of that could happen.

When I was six or seven years old, I attended a week of spiritual emphasis at a college where my father taught theology. Truthfully, there is much about the week that I *don't* remember. I do not recall who the speaker was or what he named his sermon series. I do not remember who participated in the programs or even why I, being only a child, was attending meetings intended for the college students.

But I do remember that the theme of the week was the second coming of Christ—the *soon,* the *imminent* coming of Christ.

And I remember fear. It scared me! Why was I afraid? Just as sure as I was that the coming would happen soon, I was certain that it would be awful and awesome and that I would not be ready.

In terms of the Second Advent, then, two things characterized my early years: certainty that Jesus would come and would come soon; and fear that I probably would not be ready.

The years have passed. Now I am an adult. I have graduated from college and earned three advanced degrees. I have worked in three different branches of ministry. I am married. My wife and I have two beautiful children, and we are paying off the mortgage on our home.

And Jesus hasn't come.

Knowing others who share a belief in the coming of Christ has convinced me that I am far from being alone in my experience. Many have lived through similar experiences of certainty and fear. And such experiences can create destabilizing *un*certainty. Has something gone wrong? What do we do? Do we maintain our confidence? Were we wrong about what we believed and preached? Has the coming been delayed, or was it just never as close as we thought it was?

Most who believe in the second coming of Christ have in some way been affected by such realities, and many have responded in one of two ways to the fact that Christ has not come. The first way is by *relinquishing their beliefs in the Second Advent.* "I don't want to hear it anymore," is a common refrain from those who feel both disappointed at the absence of the Advent and angered by the fire-breathing preachers of yesteryear who both scared them and scarred them in their formative years.

I spoke one day with a friend of mine who is an accomplished professional in his field. The topic turned to sermons.

We conversed for a while about the process by which preachers choose their sermon topics and what leads them to such themes. I asked him what he, as a church member, wanted to hear preached more often and what he wanted to hear less frequently. His answer was swift and unequivocal. "I don't want to hear any more sermons about the soon coming of Christ," he said rather forcefully.

I was taken aback by the heat of his remark. "Really? Why is that?" I asked.

"I grew up hearing that," he said. "We heard over and over again that Christ was coming soon, *very* soon. The time of trouble was just around the corner. It would be a terrible time. And it was about to burst forth upon us. We were scared much of the time. And yet look at me now—almost five decades later, and here I am. Christ hasn't come. And I don't want my children growing up scared like I did. So I don't want to hear any more sermons about the *soon coming* of Christ."

It is a troublesome sentiment, yet my friend is not alone in holding it. Others voice similar concerns. There are even Christian preachers who have decided that they simply will not preach on the topic of the advent of Christ, ever. It has caused so much false anticipation and anxiety and negative sentiment in the past that they do not wish to contribute to such in the present.

It is hard to fault those who make such choices. After all, how many times can the warning, "Wolf!" be sounded before it loses its power to impress? Every parent knows that regularly threatening punishment and never following through will simply assure that their children will soon cease to listen. Should we expect it to be different with the proclamation of the Advent?

There are Christians, then, who have dealt with the disappointment over the fact that we are still here by *relinquishing their beliefs in an imminent advent.*

The second way we have dealt with the fact that we are still here is by *reaffirming our traditional approach.* We not only affirm the fact that Christ is coming, and coming soon, but we continue to use the tactics of the past in announcing it.

An example of such an approach came across my desk not long ago. A concerned church member shared a copy of a fax with me. The fax announced that a certain well-known Christian organization was in the process of pressuring political figures to push forward their religiously motivated end-time agenda. If the organization succeeded, it would result in a hastening of end-time events in a way consistent with what many believe will happen just before the coming of Christ. The person who gave me the fax had a question: Could what the paper said portend the end? Was the coming of Christ *finally* just around the corner? Was this the beginning of the final, rapid moves? I have to admit, when I first read it, it brought up once again the fear and dread of my youth.

Was there something to it?

I decided not to let the matter rest. I visited the Web site of the Christian organization said to be pushing this agenda. Looking over their homepage, I noticed at the bottom of the page the word, "HOAX." Clicking on it, it opened to a page that explained that without their knowledge or consent a rumor had been making the rounds of the Christian world regarding their involvement in trying to bring about a politically enforced day and way of worship and rest. However, said the Web site, it was, quite simply, *not true.* The organization was asking for help, urging those who encountered the story to do their best to help kill it.

I wasn't surprised that the story was a hoax. After all, I have encountered many such stories over the years. But I was disturbed by the fact that we are too easily taken in by such stories. While the details and organizations may vary, the message has repeatedly been the same—*something is going on behind the scenes somewhere that portends the end. So get ready, because here it comes.* Time and again these have been false alarms.

While such stories and incidents will continue to vex us, there is, without a doubt, a positive reason for them. They remind us of the desire—the *legitimate* desire—that believers have to be in the kingdom with Christ soon! They underline the profound longing in the believer's heart for the sinful scene of our sufferings and temptations to come to a glorious end in the coming of Christ. Yet, while we must affirm such desire, we must at the same time resist the temptation to be sensationalistic in our approach. In fact, such stories and incidents suggest that we should answer some questions: Have we learned from the past? Have the false alarms of bygone years taught us any lessons? Is there another way to approach the topic of the second advent of Christ?

Certainly, relinquishing our beliefs of a returning Savior is not a satisfactory approach for the Christian, for it fails to take seriously the Word in which we believe. Christ spoke repeatedly and with unmitigated certainty of the fact that He would return. Several of His parables deal with the coming. Some of His most beloved words promise that He will indeed return. "Do not let your hearts be troubled. Trust in God; trust also in me. In my Father's house are many rooms; if it were not so, I would have told you. I am going there to prepare a place for you. And if I go and prepare a place for you, *I will come back* and take you to be with me that you also may be where I am" (John 14:1–3; italics added).

In the book of Acts, Luke tells us that as Christ's followers stood gazing up at the ascending Christ, the angels spoke to them: " 'Men of Galilee,' they said, 'why do you stand here looking into the sky? This same Jesus, who has been taken from you into heaven, *will come back* in the same way you have seen him go into heaven' " (Acts 1:11; italics added). We can only imagine the preciousness of such a promise to the members of the early church who had known Christ personally. *Their Jesus* would come again! They would be reunited *with Him*! The kingdom would be finally and fully realized.

The apostles affirm and reaffirm the reality of Christ's promised return. Paul is unequivocal: "For *the Lord himself will come down from heaven,* with a loud command, with the voice of the archangel and with the trumpet call of God, and the dead in Christ will rise first. After that, we who are still alive and are left will be caught up together with them in the clouds to meet the Lord in the air. And so we will be with the Lord forever. Therefore encourage each other with these words" (1 Thessalonians 4:16–18; italics added). Paul also reassures us, "Listen, I tell you a mystery: We will not all sleep, but *we will all be changed*—in a flash, in the twinkling of an eye, *at the last trumpet.* For the trumpet will sound, the dead will be raised imperishable, and we will be changed" (1 Corinthians 15:51, 52; italics added). And he tells Titus that how we live matters, since, after all, we are waiting "for the blessed hope—*the glorious appearing* of our great God and Savior, Jesus Christ" (Titus 2:13; italics added).

Not to be outdone, James tells his readers to "be patient . . . until the Lord's coming" (James 5:7). And John, in his first epistle, tells us in words so simple as to be breathtaking that what Jesus has promised us is nothing less than eternal life (see 1 John 2:25). This eternal life is to be bestowed at the time of the resurrection at the coming of Christ (see John 5:28, 29).

And we would be remiss to overlook that final book of Scripture, the Revelation. This sometimes disturbing, sometimes baffling book brims with the expectation of a Lord who will return to set up a kingdom that (in the words of Daniel, the Old Testament prophet) "will never be destroyed" (2:44). "Look, *he is coming* with the clouds, and every eye will see him, even those who pierced him; and all the peoples of the earth will mourn because of him. So shall it be! Amen" (Revelation 1:7; italics added). Also in Revelation we find that most precious of promises, that God " 'will wipe every tear from their eyes. There will be no more death or mourning or crying or pain, for the old order of things has passed away. . . . Write this down, for these words are trustworthy and true' " (Revelation 21:4, 5).

I have quoted merely a smattering of the words of biblical writers regarding the Second Advent. In the light of such evidence, it is unacceptable for us to approach the theme of the advent of Christ with avoidance or neglect. If we wish to be biblically sound in our theology, we simply cannot relinquish our beliefs in the Advent. Scripture is replete with the doctrine. How then can Christians safely avoid it?

Relinquishing our belief in the Advent fails to take Scripture seriously enough. However, the second approach—*reaffirming our traditional approach*—is unsatisfactory as well, for it fails to take seriously enough the world in which we live.

Believers have at times read into every event of the world— from the most mundane to the most spectacular—a sign of the end. A war breaks out, and it is viewed as a sign of the end. Famines, an earthquake, a political upheaval, or a movie with submerged religious themes come along, and they are all taken as signs of the end. In certain extreme examples, any and every random event is understood to foreshadow a swift-coming end. It is true that Christ spoke of such signs, yet the repetitive and seemingly endless nature of such events belies the possibility that each and every one of them, over a long span of time, presages an immediate end. Furthermore, viewing the world in such a way tends to make us less responsive to the needs around us and less responsible for doing what we can to improve the world in which we currently live.

Christians are correct to place strong emphasis on the coming of Christ, the end of the world, and the creation of a new world. However, forgetting that we are yet citizens of *this* world, and that *this* world came from the Creator's hand, and that *this* world, though marred, still retains the fingerprints of its Creator, can cause us to live as mere tenants, unconcerned about the place we inhabit. After all, with such a view, it is not our responsibility to pay for its upkeep.

While both of these approaches to the advent of Christ are unsatisfactory, they are nevertheless understandable. On the one hand, it is not hard to understand why some Christians have grown weary of hearing the same message time and again without the desired result. This is particularly true when the methods by which the coming has been proclaimed have at times been wild-eyed and sensationalistic, leading to fear and dread. This is especially true for those who grew up hearing and rehearsing the message of an imminent advent. Admittedly, if such a message were framed in the context of a fully orbed gospel—relating to real life with its needs, demands, joys, sorrows, realities, and wants—the ultimate effect is less likely to be negative. If not, it is disturbing to repeatedly consider a reality that (we're told) should be joyful, and yet causes us to experience great fear. And then, to hear it time and again and yet have it never happen, can ultimately become unbearable. So while the approach of relinquishing our belief in the Advent is misguided, it is not without reason. It makes sense.

On the other hand, for more than two thousand years Christians have longed for Christ to return to finally and fully inaugurate His kingdom. It is the blessed hope that has "beat eternal" in the breast of countless Christian believers. It has sustained them through good times and bad; through trial, persecution, and fire; through dark ages of travail and centuries of neglect by the surrounding society. It has stoked the fires of faith in otherwise cold and clammy cultures. It has given Christians a goal on which to focus. It has assured believers that history is indeed going somewhere, and that God's ways of love and justice will finally win the day. Because of that, it is no wonder that Christians have been quick—sometimes *too* hasty—to proclaim that the end is just around the corner. It explains why Christians have been repetitive and even relentless in their proclamation that Jesus is coming soon.

So, while some of the methods have been misguided and some of the emphasis misplaced, it is nevertheless understandable. We want to see Jesus! We wish to be with Him! We long for a world where sin is a distant and quickly fading memory. And we wish it to happen soon! It is easy to understand the reason behind the emphasis on the coming. But sometimes it has resulted in misguided methods and views.

If, then, these two approaches are unsatisfactory, is there another way? Is there a way that allows us to take seriously both the Word in which we believe and the world in which we live?

Maybe there is. And maybe the best way to discover that option comes through scrutinizing a well-known, but not always well-understood, section of Matthew's Gospel. It is only one of the many places where the New Testament speaks of the coming of Christ but is rich in detail. In fact, it is the most complete record of Christ's own teaching regarding His coming and preparation for it.

Matthew's Gospel contains the preaching of Jesus in five discourses. In each discourse, Jesus preaches on themes that will forever after be of vital importance to His followers. The first discourse, Matthew 5:1–7:29, is what we have commonly called The Sermon on the Mount. Its substance is Jesus' theology of the law of the new kingdom. It is among the most well known and loved of Jesus' teachings.

The second discourse, Matthew 10:5–11:1 comes at the time Jesus sends out the apostles on their mission. Its focus is, understandably, on mission and martyrdom. Christ's servants for ages to come would find these words of great value.

The third discourse, Matthew 13:1–53, turns its eye toward a fuller understanding of the kingdom of God. Jesus accomplished this through telling what are often called "the parables of the kingdom." The parables of the sower, the weeds, the mustard seed, and others help Christ's disciples in all ages to understand His kingdom more fully.

The fourth discourse, Matthew 18:1–19:2, considers life under the authority of the kingdom. It deals with themes such as what is most highly valued in the kingdom of God, and how to live as true disciples of that kingdom.

The final discourse, Matthew 24:1–25:46 will be the focus of our attention in this book. In this discourse Jesus deals with the topic of His return, what will precede it, and how to prepare for it. It is the section of the Gospel containing the most condensed and thorough teachings of Christ on His return and preparation for it.[1]

It just may be that in these words and teachings we will discover a meaningful third option, another way of relating to the certainty that the end is near again.

---

[1] These divisions of Matthew are drawn from D. A. Carson, *The Expositor's Bible Commentary* (Grand Rapids, Mich.: Zondervan, 1984), 8:51–57.

CHAPTER TWO

Put Down the Trumpet!

Not long into the events of Tuesday, September 11, 2001, a conviction began to build within me. While watching planes explode, buildings collapse, and people die; while listening to heads of state and people on the street and reporters; while trying to think about how this would affect our world; while that jumble of realities swirled within me, a conviction began to build: *The time of the end is here. Again.*

Richard Kyle wrote a book entitled, *The Last Days Are Here Again: A History of the End Times.*[1] Though written prior to the events of 9/11, his title expresses a sentiment similar to mine. Other people who viewed the events that day reported having much the same conviction. The end is near. Again. It's a solemn, sobering realization.

In the days following September 11, conversations took place in which Christians wondered aloud whether the mess this old planet has gotten itself into has finally gone so far as to have no human solution. Has the time finally come when we are to seriously lift up the trumpet? You do remember the words to that old hymn, don't you? Most of us have not sung it in quite some time:

> Lift up the trumpet,
> And loud let it ring:
> Jesus is coming again!
> Cheer up, ye pilgrims, be joyful and sing;
> Jesus is coming again!
> Coming again, coming again,
> Jesus is coming again![2]

It is a hymn that *I* sang over and over again in my formative years. I listened to many sermons, participated in many Bible studies, and got in on many discussions that promised beyond any reasonable doubt, "Jesus is coming again. And He's coming soon, *very* soon, *sooner than you can imagine.*"

But year after year and decade after decade of waiting has caused the edge to wear off, the anticipation to cool, and the hope to dissipate. Consequently, the prospect of discussing the imminent second advent of Christ produces different responses.

For a few, the response is, "Yes! The blessed hope! It's about time we talk more about it!" But, for others, there is a stretch, a yawn, and a question of what's next on the agenda. And some even wonder, "When are we going to learn to just leave it alone and let it happen whenever it will?" If we are honest, even the most fervent among us has to admit it: "I've heard it all my life. And yet, here I am in the early days of the twenty-first century, and He hasn't come yet." But then September 11 happens, and we intuitively know it: the time of the end is here again.

So, what do we do? How do we respond?

May I suggest that we just *put down the trumpet*? Go ahead! Put it down for a little while and let's just talk. Let's talk about the fact that the time of the end is here again. It is obvious that many have questions about the last days. And the questions we have are not new. We are not even the first ones to ask them. No, they were asked a long time ago by the disciples of old.

One day, near the end of His ministry, as Jesus was leaving the temple, His disciples came up to Him to call His attention to its buildings.

> "Do you see all these things?" he asked. "I tell you the truth, not one stone here will be left on another; every one will be thrown down." As Jesus was sitting on the Mount of Olives, the disciples came to him privately. "Tell us," they said, "when will this happen, and what will be the sign of your coming and of the end of the age?" (Matthew 24:1–3).

August 9, 1998, found me in the Arizona desert traveling north on Interstate 17 with a friend. We were driving from Phoenix to Flagstaff. The route has a divided highway with a large median separating the northbound and southbound sides of the highway. It snakes through the desert with very little shoulder on either side of the road and only very occasional exits. The desert pressing in on the highway is rough and wild and rocky, *not* to be driven on.

At a certain point in our trip, we noticed an accident on the southbound side of the highway. (We later discovered that it was a fatal crash.) From the point where the accident had occurred, cars were backed up in the two southbound lanes. At first we didn't pay much attention, though we did notice that the other side of the freeway looked like a parking lot. However, as we continued to drive, we were amazed to see that the cars were solid—in both lanes—for a mile, and then for two miles, and then for four miles. Solid cars. Nobody moving, nobody *able* to move. Eight miles, ten miles, twelve miles, just car after car after car. Fifteen miles. Twenty miles. People were sitting on hoods, lying on roofs, camped beside the road. They could not get off the road, could not go forward or backward. There was nothing to do but wait.

When we turned off the highway something over twenty miles down the road, the traffic jam still stretched into the distance. We later learned that it went on for many more miles!

I can imagine that there were two predominant questions on the lips of those stranded motorists: *What?* and *When?*

What happened? What's the hold-up? What needs to take place to get us moving again? What are we going to do?

And, *when? When* will they take care of this? When will we ever get to a place with water? And food? And a restroom? When will we get home?

The disciples of old, having just heard Jesus say that the temple—that magnificent structure on which their hopes centered—would come tumbling down, came to Jesus with two basic questions: *When?* and *What? When* will You come? and *What* will be the signs that Your coming is near? The disciples are not alone in asking these questions. We have joined them time and time again. One friend suggests that what the disciples want is a calendar and a clock. "Tell us," they ask, "when and what?"[3]

One of the reasons we ask these questions is that we human beings are curious creatures. A little girl is said to have asked question after question of her mother until her mother finally lost all patience with her and said, "Don't you know that curiosity killed the cat?"

That stopped the little girl dead in her tracks . . . for a few seconds! Then she asked, "Mommy, what did the cat want to know?"

We are often like that little girl. Curious. So we ask *When?* But we have a penchant not only for asking the question, but also for trying to provide the answer. And that creates an immediately recognizable problem: *we have always been wrong.* As a result, many do not want to hear about the end time anymore. So maybe we had better put down the trumpet and consider what our dealing with this question of *when* has been like.

A brief glimpse of history shows that the church has often been certain it knew exactly *when* Christ would come. The years A.D. 500 and A.D. 1000 were set as dates for His coming, as was also the year 1260. Later, the year 1533—the fifteenth centennial of Christ's death—was said to be the date. And so, too, were 1843, 1844, 1845, 1847, 1851, and 1914.

And there have been well-known names involved with trying to answer the question "*When?*" Listen to these words:

It is certain from the Holy Scriptures that we have no more temporal things to expect. All is fulfilled. The Roman Empire is at an end, the Turk has reached his highest point, the pomp of the papacy is falling away, and the world is cracking on every side as if it would fall apart.[4]

Do these words sound modern to you? Change the names and they could have been written last September. Especially that last line, "the world is cracking on every side as if it would fall apart."

Yet Martin Luther wrote them in 1530. And Jesus did not return. Luther must have learned this lesson well because just three years later he rebuked an opponent named Stifel for predicting that the second coming of Christ would happen at 8:00 A.M. on October 19, 1533![5]

If the history of the church has taught us anything about the question of *when*, it has taught us this: *maybe we had better put down the trumpet.*

Consider more recent times. In my formative years, a story about a vanishing hitchhiker made the rounds. As the story went, a Christian man picked up a hitchhiker, who climbed into the backseat of his car. As they drove, the topic of their conversation turned to the soon coming of Christ. Rather abruptly, the hitchhiker said, "Jesus is coming soon, *far sooner* than you Christians believe." Startled by the certainty of the statement, the driver turned to look at the hitchhiker. When he did so, the hitchhiker had vanished and the back seat was covered with blood. I still remember the alarm I felt at hearing of the proximity of the Advent in that story.

Have you ever heard that story? If so, you might be interested in these words, taken from Jon Paulien's book, *What the Bible Says About the End-Time:*

In 1981 Jan Brunvand's book *The Vanishing Hitchhiker* appeared in print. In it he discusses what he calls "urban legends," and among them is the story of a hitchhiker who proclaims that Jesus is returning soon and then disappears. Variations on this story . . . can be traced all the way back to the late 1800s. . . . Researcher Lydia M. Fish of the State University College of New York at Buffalo has cataloged some 60 stories about a disappearing hitchhiker who announced an imminent Second Advent.[6]

It is, quite simply, an urban legend. Maybe we'd better put down the trumpet.

Have these attempts to answer the *when* question touched the Seventh-day Adventist Church? Consider: Two professors at the Seventh-day Adventist Theological Seminary at Andrews University have catalogued no fewer than twenty attempts in Adventist history to set a date for the coming of Christ.[7] And yet, despite our fascination with and our attempts to answer the *when* question, we are still here. Such answers have failed to produce the Advent.

A woman tells of the visit to her home of her missionary aunt and uncle and their children, one of which was a little boy. When the missionary children were called in for dinner their mother said, "Be sure to wash your hands."

Their little boy—just a young tyke—scowled and muttered, "Germs and Jesus. Germs and Jesus. That's all I hear, and I've never seen either one of them!"[8]

If you've ever felt that way, then you are probably saying, *"Maybe we'd better put down the trumpet."* When is Christ coming? The disciples asked it. And we continue to ask it.

But *when* is not the only question the disciples asked. They also asked, "*What?*" "*What* will be the signs that will let us know that Your coming is near? *What* will alert us to the fact that it's almost here?"

There is great interest surrounding this topic. Hollywood has produced a variety of movies dealing with end-time scenarios. Movies such as *Deep Impact, End of Days, Armageddon, Omega Code, Strange Days,* and many others suggest not only religious but even secular apocalypses.

Not too long ago, *Newsweek* did a cover story on prophecy. Hal Lindsey's book, *The Late Great Planet Earth* is said to have been the best-selling nonfiction book between 1970 and 1980. The current series written by Tim LaHaye and Jerry Jenkins, *Left Behind,* has sold millions of copies. One of the common threads in these and other books and movies is that of being able to delineate exactly *what* it is that will happen leading up to the end of the world, and the coming of Christ.

Sometimes such approaches border on the ridiculous. Some will go to unusual lengths to fix the identity of the antichrist. Take for example the person who said that former president Ronald Reagan was the antichrist because he had six letters in each of his three names: Ronald Wilson Reagan.[9] In the same vein, consider that he had a deadly wound, and that it was healed! Unfortunately for the theory, and tragically for its target, this "antichrist" now has Alzheimer's.

The Christian church, in fact, appears to have taken what Jesus says in Matthew 24 and made a cottage industry from it. We have been prone to taking almost any unusual event and saying, "It's a sign of the end." Can you still recall some of the hoopla and hysteria that accompanied Y2K? It has, at times, reached a state of confusion that is unhealthy and extreme.

The disciples asked, "When?" and they asked, "What?" And so do we.

Matthew 24 tells us how Jesus responds to the disciples' questions. His answers are actually quite simple, though somewhat disconcerting.

To the *when* question He simply says, "No one knows" (see Matthew 24:36). And to the *what* question He lays out a variety of different signs. Many of them are, in a certain sense, generic. That is, they've happened continuously from His day to ours. And they don't give us the answer to the *when* question.

So, we have a problem. We do not get the answers we really want to hear. Instead, Jesus' answers just add to our distress. His first two words in the New International Version, in answer to the disciples' questions are, "Watch out!" In the New Revised Standard Version, the word is, "Beware!" Neither option is particularly comforting!

I wonder why He didn't just answer their questions.

In a sense He *does* answer, and His answer is: "*Be ready!* Since you don't know when, *always* be ready." But He doesn't answer in the way we wish He would. But why?

Could it be that He thought that knowing the answer might not be in our best interest? Could it be that Christ knew that a spiritual experience dependent upon *when* and *what* is a troubled, sporadic experience, an experience that lurches and staggers from one major scare to the next, being propelled unevenly forward by the fear of not being ready? Could it be that Christ is much more interested in a life that is marked by *daily faithfulness* than He is in us having the specific answers that satisfy our curiosity?

Could it be that He knew there is actually something much more important than *when?* and *what?* In fact, chapters 24 and 25 of Matthew seem to redirect the disciples' questions. Jesus refocuses their attention to the more important questions of *who?* and *how?* Maybe it's more important to know *who* we are preparing to meet and *how* to be ready to meet Him *whenever* He may choose to come.

If that's true, then there is good news. We have reason for great hope! Because Jesus *does* answer those questions! He answers the *how* question by telling four parables. Those four parables will be our focus in chapters 4 through 7.

And what about the *who* question? Well, He who speaks these words is Himself the answer to the *who* question. It is He whom we await, He who will return.

Do you know Him? He is the Jesus whose eyes, says John the revelator, are like blazing fire and on whose head are many crowns. He sits astride a galloping white stallion with the armies of heaven following after. Of Him it is said, "He will reign forever and ever." It is the Jesus on whose robe and thigh is written, "King of kings and Lord of lords." It is *that* Jesus. Do you know Him?

This is the Jesus who also said, "God so loved the world that He gave His one and only Son." This is the Jesus who said, "I came so that you might have life, and have it in abundance." This is the Jesus who said, "I no longer call you servants, but I call you friends." This is the Jesus who is *for* you, not against you, the Jesus who wants to be not only your Lord and Savior but your *Companion* and *Friend. That's* the Jesus who spoke these words; *that's* the Jesus who is coming. He is at once mighty and meek, grand and gracious, kingly and quiet. That is the Jesus whom we await.

Could I suggest to you that it is of primary importance to acquaint yourself with this multi-faceted, living and loving Lord? Because it is in knowing Him that you come to know the answers to the *who* and the *how,* rather than focusing merely on the *what* and the *when.* Then, with the right focus, we can truly and certainly lift up the trumpet!

A friend of mine whom I'll call James told me his love story back in the early days of my ministry. It was only a matter of days after his wedding to his high-school sweetheart that James shipped out for military action in Vietnam.

"I missed my wife," James told me, "more than I can ever tell you. We wrote to each other on an almost daily basis. We shared our hearts and bared our souls through our letters. We longed for the day when reunion would occur."

James did not use these specific words to describe it, but as I reflect on his story, I realize they are probably the best words to depict their experience: *When* would they see each other again, and *what* would have to happen to bring that about? *When?* and *What?*

There were two or three false alarms when he thought he was going home, and he wrote telling her. Then, when it did not happen, the disappointment was keen and deep.

They finally accepted the fact that they did not know when nor what it would take. So they focused on *who* and *how.* They carried photographs that constantly reminded them of exactly to whom their hearts belonged. And they remembered that one of the most practical ways—one of the best how-tos—of keeping their love alive was through continued communication. So they just kept writing those letters.

And then the news came again: he was going stateside. Not

able to face the prospect of another disappointment, James did not tell her this time that he might be coming home. But this time the news was for real. This time he *did* come home.

I will never forget James's face as he described that day to me. His eyes sparkled, his face gleamed, and his eyes bore right through me, as though gazing back into the front room of an old home in the south. A young serviceman quietly—almost like a thief—walks in the front door. A young wife sees him. She cries out and rushes to him. James said, "She could hardly speak for two days. All she did was hold on to me, and I to her."

Faced with the impossibility of answering *when* and *what,* they focused on *who* and *how.*

Maybe we should too. Maybe now that the end of time is here again, better than asking *"When?"* and *"What?"* is asking *"Who?"* and *"How?"*

---

[1] Richard Kyle, *The Last Days Are Here Again: A History of the End Times* (Grand Rapids, Mich.: Baker, 1998).

[2] *The Seventh-day Adventist Hymnal* (Hagerstown, Md.: Review and Herald®, 1985), 213.

[3] I am indebted to my friend and colleague, Dr. Louis Venden, for pointing out the simplicity of these two questions the disciples asked.

[4] See Endnote 5 for quotation reference.

[5] These incidents, along with Luther's words, are quoted in Michael Green, *The Message of Matthew* (Downers Grove, Ill.: InterVarsity Press, 2000), 257.

[6] Jon Paulien, *What the Bible Says About the End-Time* (Hagerstown, Md.: Review and Herald®, 1994), 20, 30.

[7] Ibid., 20.

[8] Vesper Bauer, in *Christian Reader,* Sep/Oct 1998, 11.

[9] Paulien, 20.

CHAPTER THREE

Faded Signs

A number of years ago a newspaper in southern California published the story of young mother and child who had mysteriously vanished into the desert night while on a church campout.[1] The tent was slashed, and, though nothing seemed to have been taken, the woman and child had simply disappeared. Frantic campers summoned nearby police, who launched a search. Hundreds of people combed the sandy desert and the rock-strewn ravines. Everybody feared the worst.

Nearly two weeks after the mysterious disappearance—by which time all but the most unrealistic hopes had been abandoned—the mother and her child turned up, hungry, with clothing torn to nearly nothing, matted hair, and fear in their eyes.

What had happened? Had they been victims of foul play? Was a kidnapper or a rapist on the loose? Was some other unknown perpetrator to blame? Not in this case. It was something more simple and, in reality, more troublesome.

On the night of their disappearance a disturbance on the campground had disrupted the campers' sleep. The police were called. The mother heard the ruckus and assumed that the last days were at hand. She knew she had to flee. So she slashed the tent, grabbed her young child, and vanished into the blackness of the desert night.

She saw the search parties. She heard the helicopters. But she was certain that she knew who held the flashlights and piloted those whirly birds. It was the forces of the antichrist, searching for the remnant in hiding. When her rescuers drew close, she cowered in fear and pressed herself and her child ever deeper into the crags of the rocks. It took nearly two weeks for her to realize that this was not, in fact, the end of the world. Finally, hunger and thirst drove them out of hiding.

What had happened? Was it just an eccentric woman with a trigger-happy fear? Or was there something else?

The end of time is here. Again. And, quite frankly, we have to admit that we are in bad shape. The face of international politics has not looked this grim in a long time. The economic situation causes no small stir. The threat of a world at war is not an unreasonable one. Our age is characterized by moral decadence. And the events of September 11, along with the aftermath they created, have only heightened the fear of many. Consequently, there are many who are ready to slash the tent, grab the kids, and run for cover. In fact, when reading the title to this book, some would doubtless like it better if we would change the wording to "Waiting No Longer" instead of *Waiting and Longing.*

A quotation has been making the rounds since September 11. It appears in volume nine in a series of books entitled *Testimonies for the Church,* and was written many decades ago. The chapter is entitled, "The Last Crisis," and it begins on page 12.

Here are the words:

> On one occasion, when in New York City, I was in the night season called upon to behold buildings rising story after story toward heaven. These buildings were warranted to be fireproof, and they were erected to glorify their owners and builders. Higher and still higher these buildings rose, and in them the most costly material was used. Those to whom the buildings belonged were not asking themselves: "How can we best glorify God?" The Lord was not in their thoughts. . . .
>
> As these lofty buildings went up, the owners rejoiced with ambitious pride that they had money to use in gratifying self and provoking the envy of their neighbors. Much of the money that they thus invested had been obtained through . . . grinding down the poor. They forgot that in heaven an account of every business transaction is kept; every unjust deal, every fraudulent act, is there recorded. The time is coming when in their fraud and insolence men will reach a point that the Lord will not permit them to pass, and they will learn that there is a limit to the forbearance of Jehovah.
>
> The scene that next passed before me was an alarm of fire. Men looked at the lofty and supposedly fireproof buildings and said: "They are perfectly safe." But these buildings were consumed as if made of pitch. The fire engines could do nothing to stay the destruction. The firemen were unable to operate the engines.[2]

So we have events like 9/11 and quotations like 9/11 and 12 and 13. And we are ready to slash the tent and flee into the night. Is the end here?

But, there is more. Consider the signs of which Jesus speaks in Matthew 24:4–14, 21, 22, 30, 31:

Jesus answered: "Watch out that no one deceives you. For many will come in my name, claiming, 'I am the Christ,' and will deceive many. You will hear of wars and rumors of wars, but see to it that you are not alarmed. Such things must happen, but the end is still to come. Nation will rise against nation, and kingdom against kingdom. There will be famines and earthquakes in various places. All these are the beginning of birth pains.

"Then you will be handed over to be persecuted and put to death, and you will be hated by all nations because of me. At that time many will turn away from the faith and will betray and hate each other, and many false prophets will appear and deceive many people. Because of the increase of wickedness, the love of most will grow cold, but he who stands firm to the end will be saved. And this gospel of the kingdom will be preached in the whole world as a testimony to all nations, and then the end will come. . . .

"For then there will be great distress, unequaled from the beginning of the world until now—and never to be equaled again. If those days had not been cut short, no one would survive, but for the sake of the elect those days will be shortened. . . .

"At that time the sign of the Son of Man will appear in the sky, and all the nations of the earth will mourn. They will see the son of Man coming on the clouds of the sky, with power and great glory. And he will send his angels with a loud trumpet call, and they will gather his elect from the four winds, from one end of the heavens to the other."

As we in the twenty-first century read these verses, we almost immediately recognize a problem: *it has all happened before.* As grim as things are today, we can point to multiplied times in history when things have been just as grim. Depending on where in the world you have lived, you may have experienced frightening "end-like" events more than once during your lifetime.

Have you ever asked questions like these? What must people have said to one another as the Black Death spread over Europe in the late 1340s and early 1350s? What did people think when the great earthquake shook Lisbon, Portugal in 1755? What was on people's minds as Stalin was murdering his millions in Russia in the 1930s and beyond? What must Jews in Germany have said to one another as Hitler hunted them down and consumed them by the millions in the early 1940s? Have you ever wondered what all of *those* people said? Might they have said: "It's the end of the world! It can't get any worse"? If they did indeed say such things, they certainly weren't alone. Such things have been said time and time again.

So, in reading the signs in Matthew 24, we may grow uneasy, uncomfortable, or uncertain. Yes, there *are* signs. But, if we are honest, the signs have *faded,* and it is hard to read them so clearly anymore. In fact, many have developed a rather cynical view of time and history—that it is not really going anywhere; it is just an endless round of meaningless events. Do these things of which Jesus spoke—these "signs"—really point to the coming? Or is it just pure coincidence that they happen time and again?

Such coincidences do, after all, happen. Consider one instance of such historical coincidence related to two well-known and popular presidents of the United States of America: John F. Kennedy and Abraham Lincoln.

Abraham Lincoln was elected in 1860 and John F. Kennedy was elected in 1960, one hundred years apart. Both of these presidents were concerned with the issue of civil rights. Both presidents' wives lost children through death while residing in the White House. Both were slain on a Friday before a holiday, in the presence of their wives, shot in the head from behind, while sitting with another couple. Both wives were uninjured, but held the bullet-torn heads of their husbands. Both were shot with another member of their entourage being injured, but not fatally. Lincoln was shot in Ford's Theater. Kennedy was shot in a Ford-built Lincoln.

John Wilkes Booth was born in the late 1830s; Lee Harvey Oswald was born in the late 1930s. Both assassins are known by their first, middle, and last names. Booth and Oswald were both southerners favoring unpopular ideas. Lincoln's assassin ran from the theater where he shot the president and was captured in a barn or a warehouse. Oswald ran from the warehouse where he shot the president and was captured in a theater. Booth and Oswald were both slain before a trial could be held.

Both presidents' successors were born in the year '08, one hundred years apart, had been vice presidents, had the last name Johnson, were southern Democrats, were former senators, and entered the presidency in their mid-fifties. Both successors chose not to run for reelection in '68—one hundred years apart. The names Lincoln and Kennedy each contain seven letters. The names Andrew Johnson and Lyndon Johnson each contain thirteen letters. The names John Wilkes Booth and Lee Harvey Oswald each contain fifteen letters.

Abraham Lincoln died in 1865, and Andrew Johnson died in 1875—ten years apart. John F. Kennedy died in 1963, and Lyndon Johnson died in 1973—ten years apart.

And finally, a Lincoln staffer, whose name was Kennedy, apparently advised him not to go to the theater the night he was killed. And Kennedy's secretary, whose name was Lincoln, advised him not to go to Dallas.

Amazing! A truly astonishing set of coincidences. But most would immediately agree that they are just that—coincidences that have no historical or spiritual meaning. They are merely interesting, right?

Coincidence works to explain similarities between Lincoln and Kennedy, but poses significant problems with Jesus and Matthew 24. Yes, the signs have happened before many times, and now they are happening again. Is it mere coincidence? Does history follow a circular cycle with no end in sight? Or is there some greater meaning?

A partial answer may come in understanding this chapter more clearly.

First, it is important to remember that in this chapter Jesus is dealing with two different events: the destruction of Jerusalem, and the end of the world. Reading the signs leading up to both events suggests that there is similarity in what happens before each of them. Difficult, demanding, and deceptive times precede both.

Separating the two events from each other can be instructive, though it's not necessarily easy to do. Scholars, in fact, divide the chapter somewhat differently. In general, the earlier portion of the chapter—specifically verses 4–14—might be applied to the fall of Jerusalem, while the latter part of the chapter—specifically verses 21–30—might be applied to the coming of Christ. From reading the chapter in such a way, let us focus on two general conclusions.

First, the signs that Christ gives about His coming are more about the *kind* of time that will pass than they are about the *amount* of time that will pass. They are more about *quality* of time than they are about *quantity* of time. As such, there is a certain generic nature to them that may allow them to happen again and again. Both these events involve false prophets, troubled political times, and increasing evil. These things have happened all along and will continue to happen till the coming.

It may be something like this. A physician tells a recently diagnosed patient, "I'm not sure how much time you have left. It may not be real long, or you may in fact live for some years. What I *can* tell you, however, is what to *expect* during this particular treatment. It will be hard. You'll be weak and nauseated and sick." That deals with the *kind* of time, not the *amount* of time.

Second, the signs are more about *where we are headed* than about *when we will get there.* They inform us that we are on the right path rather than how far it is to our destination.

Not long ago, our little family headed to Yosemite on vacation. We were still in Redlands, our hometown, driving down the avenue that led to the freeway on-ramp. Our minivan was loaded to the gills, and from the back seat our little girl, Miranda, asked a question. You know the question! It is the most natural question in the world for a child on a trip to ask. We would hear it again and again throughout the day. "Are we almost there?" When Miranda asked it, we had not even gotten onto the interstate yet! Right then I decided that long driving trips would probably not be a frequent part of our vacation future!

While we were on that trip we traveled some roads we did not know well, so we watched for two kinds of highway signs. The first sign of which we took notice was the kind of sign that told us how far it was to the next significant stage of our journey. "Bakersfield," the sign read, "75 miles." Or "Fresno, 60 miles." Those signs helped me to answer Miranda's question. But, by and large, that's not the kind of sign that Jesus gives us in this chapter. This stands to reason, especially since Jesus Himself said, "No one knows about the day or hour" (Matthew 24:36).

There was a second kind of sign that we watched for, especially in the parts of the trip with which we were not very familiar. We watched for highway identification signs that simply told us what highway we were on. "Interstate 5," the sign said. Or "Highway 41." These were the signs that assured us we were still on the right road, though they did not give us any direct information of how close we might be getting to our destination.

Could the signs that Jesus gives us in Matthew 24 be *that* kind of sign?[3] They tell us that we are on the right road. The road is still leading us toward a certain destination, and that destination is the coming of Christ. They may not, however, give us the information we crave in order to answer the question, "Are we almost there?"

Do you remember the words from act 5, scene 5 in Shakespeare's tragedy *Macbeth*? The word comes, "The queen is dead." And here is Macbeth's response.

> "She should have died hereafter;
> There would have been a time for such a word.
> To-morrow, and to-morrow, and to-morrow,
> Creeps in this petty pace from day to day
> To the last syllable of recorded time,
> And all our yesterdays have lighted fools
> The way to dusty death. Out, out, brief candle!
> Life's but a walking shadow, a poor player
> That struts and frets his hour upon the stage,
> And then is heard no more; it is a tale
> Told by an idiot, full of sound and fury,
> Signifying nothing."

It is the final words we need to notice. They are sometimes *our* words, describing *history.*

> "It is a tale
> Told by an idiot, full of sound and fury,
> Signifying nothing."

To those words, Jesus, in Matthew 24 says, "No, no, no! Life *has* meaning because history is *going somewhere.* And the signs I leave for you are posted all along the way, constantly telling you that you are still on the right road, you are still heading for the coming."

The repetitive nature of the signs, then, is not coincidental.

Rather, it assures us that we are moving in the direction of the kingdom. History *has* a purpose; it *has* an end, and that end will be fulfilled in the coming of Christ and the kingdom of God. So the signs tell us we're *still* on the right road, *still* headed to the coming, and they tell us that the terrain over which we will travel will get worse before it gets better.

So are false prophets, wars, famines, persecution, and the evil behind events like 9/11 signs of the times? Was the evil condition which led to the reality of statements like *Testimonies,* volume 9, beginning with page 11, a sign of the end? Yes. *Absolutely.* They are signs that tell us we are on the right road; we are on the way home.

So what do we do? What does this mean for us? Do we slash the tent and flee into the night? In the four parables we will consider, Jesus tells *specifically* what to do, and what it means for us. But for now, suffice it to say, it means simply this: *We continue the journey.* We focus our energy and our attention and our wills and our hearts on making this journey in fellowship with the Jesus who spoke these words. We dedicate ourselves more faithfully to walking with Him.

As believers we hear in these signs a call to deeper faithfulness. We read the signs and realize that we are drawing nearer to the homeland, and our hearts skip a beat, our hopes rise a notch, our anticipation sweetens. We are going home!

For those who are parents, reading these signs alerts you to the necessity of parenting not just for today or for tomorrow, but for eternity. It means doing everything possible to build into the lives of your young ones an awareness of the direction history is moving.

For godly and dedicated teachers, reading these signs means that there is a larger tomorrow for which you are called to prepare your students. The preparation in which you are privileged to participate, the preparation that readies them to face a competitive and sometimes hostile world, is of great importance. But the highway signs that remind us, "We're on the right road," "We're on our way home," also remind us that the most important preparation is that which brings students to an encounter with their God.

For those in leadership capacities who are the guardians of God's sheep: Your call is not only to provide leadership, but also to influence the sharing of the good news with people who are most ready to receive it. It is a sacred calling.

To every Christian who encounters these sometimes faded signs, we find in them a call to a renewed commitment to the Christ of history, and to the reunion we will celebrate with Him at the coming.

And for all who minister, moving through time in a vehicle called *now,* we see flashing past us the road signs identifying that we are on a journey with a destination in the kingdom of God. As our ministry touches people, we do so with the conviction strong in our hearts, *"The signs, though sometimes faded, remind us that we are on our way home."*

---

[1] I am indebted to my friend and colleague, Dr. Calvin Thomsen, for sharing this story with me. Some details have been changed to protect the innocent.

[2] Ellen G. White, *Testimonies for the Church* (Nampa, Idaho: Pacific Press® Publishing Association, 1948), 9:12, 13.

[3] This suggestion regarding highway signs is not original with me. Regrettably, I am uncertain whom to credit with first noticing it.

CHAPTER FOUR

Doing What He Asked

Have you seen the bumper sticker that says, "Jesus is coming. Look busy"? It seems a bit sacrilegious, does it not? And yet, I wonder if, before we are done with Matthew 24, we might understand where the thought behind this comes from.

In his book, *The Last Days Are Here Again,* Richard Kyle suggests that, sooner or later, somebody is going to get it right. There have been, Kyle points out, so many predictions of the imminent return of Christ, so many dates set, that someone, somewhere, sooner or later is going to get it right! So let's take Kyle up on that for a moment and just suppose that we knew that the return of Christ would happen in exactly one week. That is the date. That is the time. That is it. He will be here.

If that could be guaranteed, what would you do? How would you spend your week? What would you need to take care of? Or maybe another way to ask the question is, how would you *watch* this week? How you answer that question reveals what you understand Jesus to mean when He tells us to "watch." So what would you do?

In Matthew 24:3 we read that the disciples went to Christ and asked Him the questions, "*When* will this happen, and *what* will be the sign of your coming?" (italics added). While these are understandable and natural questions, Jesus actually appears to be more interested in answering the questions *who?* and *how?*

He does deal to some degree with the *when?* and *what?* In chapter 3, we noted that He gave us certain signs of His coming. But we also noticed that those signs may actually be much less like highway *distance* signs and much more like highway *identification* signs—that history is moving inexorably toward a certain specific conclusion.

If that is true—that we do not know how far we are from our destination—then the answer to the *how?* question becomes exceedingly important. *How* do we then spend the journey? *How* do we make certain that we are prepared for the arrival?

It is to these issues that we now turn.

Notice Matthew 24:36–44:

> "No one knows about that day or hour, not even the angels in heaven, nor the Son, but only the Father. As it was in the days of Noah, so it will be at the coming of the Son of Man. For in the days before the flood, people were eating and drinking, marrying and giving in marriage, up to the day Noah entered the ark; and they knew nothing about what would happen until the flood came and took them all away. That is how it will

be at the coming of the Son of Man. Two men will be in the field; one will be taken and the other left. Two women will be grinding with a hand mill; one will be taken and the other left.

"Therefore *keep watch,* because you do not know on what day your Lord will come. But understand this: If the owner of the house had known at what time of night the thief was coming, he would have *kept watch* and would not have let his house be broken into. So you also must *be ready,* because the Son of Man will come at an hour when you do not expect him" (italics added).

Verse 36 lays down the principle: *no one knows when the coming will happen.* And *no one* includes the angels and it includes even Jesus Himself. The definitive nature of this statement has caused people to say some pretty forceful things about it. Let me share one example. It is written by an evangelical theologian, and is a statement that must have struck a little too close to home, because it caused me to wince.

Not all have accepted this counsel. Instead of concentrating on the task, they have tried to calculate the times. Drawing on the apocalyptic prophecies from Daniel and Revelation, they have insisted that events in their own day were the fulfillment of biblical predictions and that Jesus was about to return. The fact that all previous interpretations have been falsified by the continuing "delay" of the second coming does not deter some in our own time from boldly continuing along the same path. The spiritual arrogance that presumes to pry into God's secret plan is roundly condemned by Matt. 24:36. Not even the Messiah knows when the end will occur! Not even the highest archangels are privy to the Father's intention! How foolish it is for humans to think they can play with biblical numbers and ambiguous prophecies and discover what was hidden even from Jesus![1]

Ouch! That's not even nice! But, if you read the text, he is exactly right. What is the principle? *No one knows at what day or hour*—in other words, *when*—the coming will take place. No one! That is *not* ambiguous.

The next verses give us an example of that principle. They remind us of the days of Noah. In the days of Noah a couple of things were true. First, God said something was coming and no one was sure when it would hit; and second, life went on as normal. In fact, it was in the midst of life as usual that the predicted event suddenly occurred. People were following the ordinary pursuits of life—eating, drinking, and marrying—when suddenly the Flood came and caught them by surprise. And it is clear from what Jesus says in this chapter that there are similarities between that time and what will happen at the end. Impending distress and normal life-patterns will coexist. The distress points to the end, while the normalcy of life warns that the end will be unexpected.[2]

So, the principle? *No one knows the hour of His coming.* The example? *The days before the Flood.* The admonition? Verse 42, *Keep watch!* Be on the alert.

The next two verses (43, 44) then give us an example of the need for watchfulness. You know as well as I do that the thief who breaks into your house does not call ahead and ask, "Are you going to be gone this evening? I'd like to drop by and pick up some stuff!"

No, the break-in by the thief is unexpected. The thief's main ally is surprise. Therefore, if the homeowner *does not watch,* there is the risk that the thief will show up and take whatever he or she wants.

So Jesus is underlining the need to be watchful. In fact, this chapter contains a trio of admonitions. "Watch out!" says Jesus in verse 4. "Keep watch!" He reminds us in verse 42. "Be ready!" He warns in verse 44.

All of which leads to an obvious question. In fact, concerning the coming of Christ, there may be no more important question. It is a more vital question than *when?* and a more valuable question than *what?* It is a question the answer to which must be the heartfelt task of any devoted follower of the Galilean. And if we read these two chapters in Matthew correctly, it is an obvious question. Here is the question: *How? How* do we keep watch?

Christians have answered that question about watching in a variety of different ways. One answer has been to say that watching means *charting.* We have said, "The best way to watch for the Master's return is to carefully and thoughtfully and studiously chart out end-time events. Then, once we have done so, we can know exactly *what* will happen *when.* Then we commit it to memory, and we'll be ready. We will not be caught by surprise. We *cannot* be, for we have the map."

Watching, in this sense, means charting.

Another answer we have given is that watching means *confessing.* If we are to watch adequately and accurately for the coming of Christ, then we must keep our sins currently confessed, for being ready is a matter of having all of our sins confessed up to date. Should Christ come and find us with even *one* sin unconfessed, we would be out. So, watching, here, means current confession.

A third answer is that watching means *perfection.* "We need to become perfect—become sinless," we have said. "That's where our focus must be. *That* is how we watch for His appearing. And when there is a large enough group of sinless people, He will come and take us home."

Sometimes we have answered the question not so much by what we say as by how we live. And if you watch how Christians have often lived, you would probably have to agree with a good friend of mine who says, "Watching means *adrenaline.*" In fact, he calls them, "days of adrenaline."[3] You understand that, do you not? The days of adrenaline are those days when a rush of fear and adrenaline surges through our veins in response to any awesome event that could conceivably portend the end. Then, in a rush of excitement we are driven to Scripture and other spiritual books, determined to ready ourselves for the coming of Christ.

In fact, the spiritual lives of too many Christians have been marked by the uneven spikes of the adrenaline days. Too many have lived their spiritual lives from one adrenaline rush to the next.

So we have answered the question, "How do we watch?" in a variety of ways—some simple, some complex. And, to tell the truth, most of them contain at least some kernel of truth. But interestingly enough, none of these answers are what *Jesus* suggests that we do. And some of them, especially the last one—the "days of adrenaline"—go exactly *contrary* to what Jesus says.

So what *does* Jesus say? How *should* we watch?

Note now, from Matthew 24:45–51, the first of four parables where Jesus answers our question.

"Who then is the faithful and wise servant, whom the master has put in charge of the servants in his household to give them their food at the proper time? It will be good for that servant whose master finds him doing so when he returns. I tell you the truth, he will put him in charge of all his possessions. But suppose that servant is wicked and says to himself, 'My master is staying away a long time,' and he then begins to beat his fellow servants and to eat and drink with drunkards. The master of that servant will come on a day when he does not expect him and at an hour he is not aware of. He will cut him to pieces and assign him a place with the hypocrites, where there will be weeping and gnashing of teeth."

The master leaves on a trip. And when he does, he places a servant in charge, in a position of trust. The implication is that the master will return. He does not say when or how soon, but he will. The further implication is that the servant's behavior in the master's absence will determine whether or not he is ready to meet the master upon his return.

Now, there are two choices the servant can make. He can do what he has been asked to do—provide for his fellow servants as instructed; or neglect to do it. To do what was left for him to do means he will be ready when the master returns, while neglecting to do it is to be caught unprepared.

Some theologians suggest that this is a parable primarily for spiritual leaders and pastors, for people placed in some kind of authority over the flock of God. How faithful will *we* be in doing what the Master has left for us to do? Will we faithfully provide them with spiritual food at the proper time?

In a specific sense, they are undoubtedly right: There *is* a special word here to anyone placed in a position of trusted leadership, whether that person is a pastor, a teacher, a parent, or an employer. Could there not be, however, an application beyond that to us all—to *every* person who has responded to the call of Christ? Could it be that the parable tells us that watching does not primarily consist of figuring out *when* Christ is coming, but rather, *watching means doing* whatever it is that the Master left for us to do? Watching, then, is primarily concerned with whether or not we are faithful in doing the tasks that He left for us to do. Jesus is most interested in a people who will be faithful in their duties to Him *whether or not He is present.*

That is a concept that *every* parent, *every* employer can understand, is it not?

Suppose I say to my two children, "Austin and Miranda, I'm going out, and I want your rooms clean when I return." I would be somewhat disturbed if they insisted only on continuing to ask, "But *when* are you coming back, Daddy?" Why might I be disturbed? Because my interest is not so much on them getting things done *just in time* for my return as it is on them being consistently obedient *regardless* of when I return.

Could that be what Jesus is saying? That those friends of His who are truly watching for His return are so busy with the tasks that He left for them to do that they have no cause for shame regardless of when He returns? Simply put, *watching means doing,* doing whatever it is the Master left for you to do.

At the height of World War II, Protestant theologian Dietrich Bonhoeffer was imprisoned for taking a stand against Hitler. Yet he continued to urge fellow believers to resist Nazi tyranny. A group of Christians, who believed that Hitler was the antichrist, asked Bonhoeffer, "Why do you expose yourself to all this danger? Jesus will return any day, and all your work and suffering will be for nothing."

Here is how Bonhoeffer responded: "If Jesus returns tomorrow, then tomorrow I'll rest from my labor. But today I have work to do. I must continue the struggle until it's finished."[4]

During his 1960 presidential campaign, John F. Kennedy often closed his speeches with the following story about Colonel Davenport, the Speaker of the Connecticut House of Representatives. It happened one day, in the late 1700s, when the sky over Hartford, Connecticut darkened ominously. Some of the representatives, glancing out the windows, feared the end was at hand.

"We must go!" some clamored. "We must leave!" some cried. "We must adjourn!" some called.

Quelling the outcry for immediate adjournment, Davenport rose to his feet and said, "The day of judgment is either approaching or it is not. If it is not, there is no need to adjourn. And if it is, I choose to be found doing my duty. So, bring candles that we might continue at our post."[5]

That's watching! That is how we watch for the coming of our Lord. We do whatever it is that He has called us to do. What is the call of Christ upon your life? Has He called you to develop your mind through study? Then do it to the very best of your ability. And you will be watching. Has He called you to teach the minds of your young children? Then do it with the persistent kindness of those who wish to be faithful to Christ. And you will be watching. Has He placed you in a position of leadership in your community, in your place of employment, in your church? Then do the most fair and consistent job you can. And you will be watching.

Now, if this is so simple, then whatever in the world would cause this servant to *not* be ready? After all, we have to assume that the servant had done a good job in the past or the master would not have put him in charge. So what happened? If he makes the wrong choice, why does he? Why would he fail to watch?

One possible reason has to do with power: He's been placed in a position of power, and the power just went to his head. Or it could be that he's just a good old-fashioned hypocrite—works when the boss is watching, sloughs off the rest of the time. But while those might be good reasons for his failure to watch, they are not the reason the Bible gives. The reason is found in verse 48. I like the way the King James Version states it: "My lord delayeth his coming."

"My lord delays his coming. He's been gone a long time and won't be back for a long time." And that delay changes everything for the servant. It isn't that he thinks he has no job to do. He just thinks he does not have to do it *right now.*

The last two years, when April 15 rolled around, my wife's husband has had to file tax extensions! The other day my wife said to her husband, "I think it's time we start pulling the tax info together for next year." Do you know what my wife's husband said? He said, "You must be joking! There is no need to hurry! *There is plenty of time!*"

A fable is told of three young devils on their way to this earth to finish their apprenticeship. Before making their journey to earth, they talked with Satan about their plans to tempt and ruin human beings. The adversary asked each one to outline his plans.

The first one said, "I'll tell them there's no God."

Satan said, "That won't work. Most people are at least somewhat religious."

The second one said, "I'll tell them there's no hell."

And Satan said, "That won't work. Most people know there is a consequence for evil."

And the third one said, "I'll tell them there's no *hurry.*"

And Satan said, "Go, and you'll ruin them by the thousands."

In the words of one writer, "The spirit which leads to disaster is the spirit that says, 'There's plenty of time.' "[6]

Notice that in verse 48 the servant speaks of a delay, and in verse 49 he begins to beat his fellow servants, and to eat and drink with the slackers and drunkards. If watching means doing, then it is also true that focusing on the delay can lead to laxity in the doing of our duty. Why? Because the delay happens in ordinary time. Life is going on as usual. The servant may be expecting some great thing to warn him, so that then he can jump up and get ready quickly. And that is a problem. Because the very ordinariness of life causes him not to do what he is expected to do.

A rural housewife named Fay Inchfawn, who lived long ago,

wrote these lines about her life and her expectancy of Christ returning in the ordinariness of her life.

> Sometimes, when everything goes wrong;
> When days are short and nights are long,
> When wash day brings so dull a sky,
> That not a single thing will dry.
> And when the kitchen chimney smokes,
> And when there's none so "old" as folks;
> When friends deplore my faded youth,
> And when the baby cuts a tooth.
> While John, the baby last but one,
> Clings round my skirts till day is done;
> And fat, good-natured Jane is glum
> And butcher's man forgets to come.
> Sometimes I say, on days like these
> I get a sudden gleam of bliss.
> Not on some sunny day of ease
> He'll come . . . but on a day like this.[7]

Notice those last words. It is the ordinariness of life of which Inchfawn writes. And it is in the midst of such a day that the master returns and finds the servant unprepared. He was not doing what the master had asked him to do, so he was not watching. And since he was not watching, he was not ready.

When I was young we lived in Puerto Rico. My parents bought a five-acre plot of land out in the country, and we bought some farm animals—cows, horses, chickens, and so forth. We all had chores to do. One day Dad talked to my older brother John and me before leaving for work. "Sons, there's someone important coming over for supper tonight. I want you all to do all of the chores and then get cleaned up and be ready for supper by the time I get home." We knew what we had to do—milk the cows, feed the pigeons, the dog, the cats, and the horses.

And that is where things did not quite go according to plan. It had rained that day. And while bringing the cows home, we discovered a huge mud puddle in the road. To me it looked more like a lake than a puddle! Sure, company was coming, but there was plenty of time to get ready, right?!

A game was in order. My brother John would ride by on a horse, and my friend and I would try to rope him. John would grab the rope and pull us. We would fall down, and he would drag us, screaming and laughing, right through the middle of this lake! Then we would get up, and he would come from the other direction. Ditto. More mud. It was great! (Notice the word "was." I think of that game now, and I think *yuck*!)

And the company? "My lord," which in this case was my dad, "delayeth his coming." And we kept on playing. And then, suddenly, we heard a car. *Our* car. *Dad's* car. And I'm standing in the middle of this lake! I did not know the song at the time, but if I had, I would have sung it: "Oh, sinner man, where you gonna run to?" I learned then and there exactly what Jesus meant in this parable when He said there was "weeping and gnashing of teeth"!

The end of time is here. Again. So we go back to our question. What if you knew Jesus would come next week? What would you do? How would you watch this week?

If you are watching as this first parable tells us to, *if you are doing* what the Master left for you to do, could I be so bold as to suggest this? If you knew Jesus would arrive next week, your heart would pound faster, your hopes would soar higher, your joy would know no bounds, and *you would simply continue to do what you have been doing all along.* Why? Because you have already been doing the Master's bidding. And watching means doing the Master's bidding.

---

[1] Douglas R. A. Hare, *Interpretation: Matthew* (Louisville, Ky.: John Knox, 1993), 281,282.

[2] D. A. Carson makes this point in *The Expositor's Bible Commentary* (Grand Rapids, Mich.: Zondervan), 8:509.

[3] I am indebted to my friend and colleague, Dr. Earnest Schwab, for this concept.

[4] *Our Daily Bread,* November 10, 1991, found in http://www .sermonillustrations.com/a-z/r/rapture.htm, November 1, 2002.

[5] Harry Heintz, found in http://www.sermonillustrations.com/a-z/s/second _coming.htm, November 1, 2002.

[6] William Barclay, *The Daily Study Bible: The Gospel of Matthew,* revised edition (Philadelphia: Westminster Press, 1975), 2:317.

[7] Source unknown, found in http://www.sermonillustrations.com/a-z/r /rapture.htm, November 1, 2002.

CHAPTER FIVE

It's Who We Know

Sleeping when we should be watching can be dangerous. There are many examples of that simple truth. If we asked a military person about it, that soldier might say, "If I fall asleep while on guard duty, I risk any number of things—a court martial, a surprise attack by the enemy, my own death, or even the deaths of my comrades."

If we asked a truck driver about it, he might say, "If I fall asleep while driving, I endanger the lives of every other person on the road. It's surely true," he would say, "that sleeping when we should be watching can be dangerous."

Consider the case of Cecil Hicks, Orange County, California, Superior Court Judge. According to the *Orange County Register*, in May of 1998, Judge Hicks declared a mistrial in a murder case. Defendant Omar Coyotzin was accused of fatally wounding a woman during a robbery. During the trial, said the lawyers on the case, they realized that something was wrong when the judge failed to rule on a defense motion.

The problem? An embarrassed judge had to admit that he had fallen asleep. "It has never happened to me before," he said. "I think it is due to a new medication I am taking for back problems." The result? A mistrial.

It can be problematic to sleep when one should be watching.

The disciples certainly found that out, right? One famous scene in Scripture takes place in the Garden of Gethsemane the night before the crucifixion of Christ. We see Christ bending over the sleeping forms of the disciples, gently shaking them awake. "Can you not watch with Me one hour? Watch and pray, so that you don't fall into temptation." But once again they slept. First they slept, and then they failed.

Maybe for that reason the parable is unusually arresting. For at the beginning of Matthew 25, we read a story where people are supposed to be watching—in fact, Jesus ends the story by telling those listening *to watch*—and yet instead of watching, they sleep. The most interesting thing of all, however, is that *they apparently suffer no negative consequences* for their sleeping! In other words, they discover that sleeping when you should be watching may not be that big a problem. That paradox brings us once again to the question: What does it mean to watch?

The next parable that Jesus tells is the well-known parable of the ten virgins. It is found in Matthew 25:1–13.

> "At that time the kingdom of heaven will be like ten virgins who took their lamps and went out to meet the bridegroom. Five of them were foolish and five were wise. The foolish ones took their lamps but did not take any oil

with them. The wise, however, took oil in jars along with their lamps. The bridegroom was a long time in coming, and they all became drowsy and fell asleep.

"At midnight the cry rang out: 'Here's the bridegroom! Come out to meet him!'

"Then all the virgins woke up and trimmed their lamps. The foolish ones said to the wise, 'Give us some of your oil; our lamps are going out.'

" 'No,' they replied, 'there may not be enough for both us and you. Instead, go to those who sell oil and buy some for yourselves.'

"But while they were on their way to buy the oil, the bridegroom arrived. The virgins who were ready went in with him to the wedding banquet. And the door was shut.

"Later the others also came. 'Sir! Sir!' they said. 'Open the door for us!'

"But he replied, 'I tell you the truth, I don't know you.'

"Therefore keep watch, because you do not know the day or the hour."

Notice first of all the punch line in the last verse. It is the lesson of the story, and it is a warning. "Keep watch!" Why? "Because you do not know the day or the hour when the bridegroom will return. So keep watch! Be always ready."

Is Jesus not saying, "Sleeping when you should be watching could be dangerous"?

In this story, Jesus portrays a wedding where the focus is not on the bride, but rather is on the bridesmaids.[1] When we look in on the wedding and see the bridesmaids, all looks well. They are ready for the ceremony. They are dressed alike, they all have lanterns, they are excited, and they are waiting for the arrival of the bridegroom. When he arrives, they will accompany him on his procession to claim his bride.

But all is *not* well. There is trouble at the ceremony. In Matthew 25:2 Jesus says, "Five of them were foolish and five were wise." Jesus has to tell us this because we cannot tell by merely looking at them. To *any* observer, they all look the same. And yet, if five are foolish and five are wise, clearly some kind of trouble lies ahead.

So what makes the difference? What makes one bridesmaid foolish and another bridesmaid wise? What does foolishness look like to you? Does it look like a giddy teenager who giggles all the time? Or does it look like a man who is more concerned with Christian Dior than with Christian devotion?

And what does wisdom look like to you? To me, wisdom looks like a stately, elderly man. His silver-streaked hair and gray-flecked beard frame a deeply lined face. His eyes are deep pools, reflecting a life of learning. He has lived, he has learned, he knows. He is wise. That's what wisdom looks like to me. What about to you?

Actually, a more important question is, what do foolishness and wisdom look like to Jesus? He is, after all, the One telling the story. And we must ask Him that question because when we look at the ten bridesmaids, even though we know that five are foolish and five are wise, we cannot tell them apart! Both groups are at the wedding, both groups are dressed alike, and both groups are carrying lamps. On the outside, at least, as far as we can tell, everything looks the same.

"So, Jesus, what's the difference?"

If we are to understand what for Jesus comprises the difference between foolishness and wisdom, we must note one phrase in verse 5: "The bridegroom was a long time in coming." A long time. So there was a delay, and that created a problem, because it was the *delay* that would differentiate between the foolish bridesmaids and the wise ones. Notice that if the bridegroom had appeared when he was expected to appear, *all* the bridesmaids would have been ready, and thus we would have thought that they were *all* wise. But because the bridegroom delayed, we come to realize that five are foolish.

Now you understand that a delay at a wedding can cause significant problems. I experienced the truth of that firsthand. It has been long enough ago now that most of the feelings of embarrassment and desperation have worn off, but those feelings were acute then. My wife and I got a bit of a late start setting off for the wedding, but not enough to make much difference. Then we ran into another problem. We were unfamiliar with the location. There was one turn—what turned out to be one *crucial* turn—that had not been made clear on the set of directions we had. I was the minister. It was an evening wedding, set to begin at 7:00 P.M. Just after 6:30, I realized things were *not* going well.

"This sure doesn't look to me like it's where we're supposed to be," I told Anita. I drove faster and faster. But I discovered something: When you don't know where you're going, even speed doesn't help!

I kept looking at the digital clock on the dashboard—6:45, 6:50, 6:55. *Desperation.* 7:05. 7:10. "Where is a police officer when you need one?" It was almost 7:20 when I finally spotted a police car. I leaped out and ran up to him and quickly explained my predicament. Could he give me directions? He thought it was funny. He laughed! (I felt like backhanding him.) But he gave me directions.

It was 7:30 when we finally squealed to a stop at the wedding venue. We were a full half-hour late! The bride was standing at the door looking as though she had swallowed a golf ball that got stuck halfway down. A delay at a wedding does those kinds of things to people. And a delay at the wedding in Matthew did certain things to the bridesmaids, as well.

Likewise, a lengthy wait for Christ's coming has affected His church. From a human perspective, the coming has been delayed beyond anyone's expectation. Read the New Testament! The early Christians expected Christ to come almost immediately. But two thousand years later, we are still waiting. And we are acutely aware of the delay even in our own lifetime.

My mom and dad tell me that when Dad completed ministerial studies at Union College in Lincoln, Nebraska, they went straight to the mission field, side-stepping seminary at that time, because the coming of Christ was just too close. That was almost half a century ago.

When I graduated from college, I wondered about the closeness of the coming. I seriously considered whether or not I should proceed to seminary or just go straight to work in the vineyard of the Lord, helping to prepare others for His coming. That was more than twenty years ago.

A family I knew listened to a set of tapes on which a preacher predicted an imminent advent of Jesus. It so affected them that they sold their possessions and moved to the country. That was almost twenty-five years ago.

"Christ is at the door!" We have heard it all our lives. And here we are today, waiting.

It is worth noting that in each of Christ's first two parables there is a surprise. In the parable discussed in the previous chapter, the servant was surprised by the arrival of his master. In this parable, the bridesmaids are surprised by the arrival of the groom. But in each case the surprise is not that the master or the groom came *sooner* than was expected. No, the surprise is that the master and the groom returned *later* than was expected. The surprise was the *delay!* Whatever distinguishes the foolish bridesmaids from the wise has to do with how they handle the delay.

So how *do* they handle it? By falling asleep. *Ten* of them fall asleep—foolish and wise alike. How can *that* be? Is it not true that sleeping when we should be watching could be dangerous? And remember, the punch line of the parable is "keep watch." So what is going on?

First we can say this: *It is possible to be both wise and asleep; it is also possible to be both asleep and ready* for the arrival of the bridegroom. So apparently when Jesus tells us to watch He does not automatically mean that watching means staying awake.

But how do we balance that against other New Testament incidents of people sleeping when they should be watching? The disciples slept when they should have been watching and praying the night before the Crucifixion, and *that* story does not end well. And Paul tells the Romans (see 13:11), "Now it is high time to awake out of our sleep, for now is our salvation nearer than when we first believed." How do passages such as those relate to the ten sleeping maidens?

Could it be that Jesus knew His church could not always live in the heat of anticipation, standing on the tiptoe of expectation?

Did He know that such a manner of living our spiritual lives would exhaust and frustrate us? Did He know that the time would come when we would sleep? And yet, could it also be that He knew we could *still be ready?* How could we still be ready? Simply this way: *by being wise.*

It becomes vital, then, to know what it means to be wise. Maybe the difference between foolishness and wisdom can be more clearly noted if we consider certain wedding customs of the day. It was very important to follow appropriate wedding etiquette. In fact, rabbis would even release their students from lectures, or exempt people from certain ritual obligations, in order to allow them to participate appropriately in wedding celebrations.[2]

New Testament commentator William Barclay quotes J. Alexander Findlay in describing such wedding celebrations. Here Findlay describes a wedding in modern-day Palestine:

"When we were approaching the gates of a Galilean town," he writes, "I caught sight of ten maidens gaily clad and playing some kind of musical instrument, as they danced along the road in front of our car; when I asked what they were doing, the [driver] told me that they were going to keep the bride company till her bridegroom arrived. I asked him if there was any chance of seeing the wedding, but he shook his head, saying in effect: 'It might be tonight, or tomorrow night, or in [several nights]; nobody ever knows for certain.' Then he went on to explain that one of the great things to do, if you could, at a middle-class wedding in Palestine, was to catch the bridal party napping. So the bridegroom comes unexpectedly, and sometimes in the middle of the night; it is true that he is required by public opinion to send a man along the street to shout: 'Behold! The bridegroom is coming!' but that may happen at any time; so the bridal party have to be ready to go out into the street at any time to meet him, whenever he chooses to come. . . . [In addition] no one is allowed on the streets after dark without a lighted lamp, and [once] the bridegroom has . . . arrived, and the door has been shut, late-comers to the ceremony are not admitted."[3]

If the bridesmaids *knew* that they could not say for certain when the groom would arrive, would it not be *foolish* to make no preparation for what could possibly be a long wait?

Do you wish to see the difference between the wise and the foolish bridesmaids? You can see it if you peer carefully into the night. There you see ten maidens fumbling frantically with the dying wicks of their lamps. But you notice that five have made preparation for this moment. They pour extra oil into their lamps, the flames flash in the night, and they are ready to meet the bridegroom! The other five are frantic—their flames have flickered and died. And at that moment we see the difference between the wise and the foolish maidens: *The foolish ones do not have extra oil.* Though they realized the wait for the groom could be long, they went to the wedding planning on it taking place very soon. Their supply of oil would only last long enough for the fulfillment of immediate expectations. Anything longer than that, and they were in serious trouble. In other words, they were ready if the bridegroom came *now;* they would not be ready if the bridegroom's arrival required a sustained tarrying time.

70

Can you imagine the panic the foolish maidens must have felt at that moment? I certainly can! When I was a freshman in college, I felt that kind of panic at the end of the first week of school. It had been a busy week, so Saturday morning I decided to sleep a bit later than usual. Not too late, though, because I had a big part in the first college Sabbath School program of the year, and it began at 9:40.

I rolled over in bed and slowly opened my eyes to check the time. I want you to picture it: The program began at 9:40, we lived several miles out of town, I had a digital clock, and it said . . . *9:41!*

It is hard to capture the frantic frenzy of what happened next. I leaped out of bed and landed in my pants! A mad dash through the bathroom hit the high spots—water on my hair, toothpaste. Then a shirt, a tie, and a coat. I drove madly, prayed, and got dressed all at the same time. And (can you believe this?) I walked onto the platform, fully dressed—suit and tie and hairstyle too—while everyone was singing the opening hymn. I looked at the clock on the back wall, and it said *9:50!* From pillow to pulpit in nine minutes. That record will never be beaten!

So I understand the frantic frenzy of the foolish maidens. It is late, and they suddenly realize that they are not prepared. They need more oil.

One theologian suggests that we learn two lessons from the foolish maidens at this critical moment. First, we learn that there are some things you have to do for yourself. No one else can do them for you, and no one else can give them to you. And second, there are some things you simply cannot acquire at the last minute. They require time to secure. And both of these realities are true of the oil.[4]

The foolish maidens were not *watching,* so they are caught unprepared.

Now, the parable itself does not tell us the specific meaning of the oil. Therefore, some see no particular meaning in it at all—it was just one of the elements needed for the processional to the house of the bride. However, if we look elsewhere in the Scriptures, we discover that there are times when oil is used symbolically of the Holy Spirit. If we assign that meaning to the oil in this parable, it becomes even more interesting to notice the groom's statement to the foolish maidens. "I don't know you," were his words. "I don't *know* you." (See Matthew 25:12.)

Is that just a way of saying, "I'm sorry, but you can't come in"? Is it just a way of saying, "You should have made better preparation"? Is it just a way of saying, "It's not enough to bring a lamp, you must also bring an adequate supply of oil"? Or is there possibly something deeper? Could the words spoken by the groom possibly be suggesting something about a deeper quality of relationship between a heavenly groom and his earthly bride, a relationship that is long lasting when the oil of the Spirit abides in the heart? Could it be suggesting the same reality about which Jesus prayed for His disciples when He requested "That they might *know* You, the only true God, and Jesus Christ whom You have sent"? (See John 17:3.)

A young management trainee spent the day with an experienced administrator as part of his training. On that particular day the administrator was interviewing applicants for a position. The trainee sat in the corner and watched. The first applicant came in, and the administrator asked him, "How much is two plus two?"

"Four."

The administrator then looked at the trainee and said, "Notice the precision, the confidence, and accuracy." Then he said to the applicant, "Wait outside."

The next applicant came in, and he asked him the same question. "How much is two plus two?"

"Six."

"Wait outside," the administrator said to the applicant. "Amazing!" he said to the trainee. "Notice the imagination, the vision, the creativity."

Then the last applicant came in. "How much is two plus two?"

"Eight."

"Magnificent! What scope, what 'outside-the-box' thinking! Wait outside."

The administrator turned to the trainee and asked, "Which one should I hire?"

The trainee did not know what to say, but he knew the administrator had been more enthusiastic about the bigger answer, so he said, "The man who said eight."

"No," the administrator said, "I will hire the one who said six."

"Why?"

"Simple. He's my wife's nephew!"

Truly, *"it's all in who you know"* is also true when it comes to waiting and watching for the coming of the Bridegroom. *It's all in who you know.*

What makes the wise *wise* and allows them to persevere is that they *know* the Groom. How does one do that? Knowing the Groom is done by maintaining a regular supply of oil, maintaining an ongoing infilling and indwelling of the Holy Spirit, regardless of whether or not the Groom arrives when expected.

And what makes the foolish *foolish* is their having only enough oil if the coming of the Bridegroom happens *now.* They are foolish because they have only enough oil for the excitement that prevails when they *think* he will arrive. But if there is a delay, then life goes back to normal, and there is no ongoing walk with Christ. Spiritually speaking, that is foolishness.

The end of time is here. Again. In these turbulent times we hear vibrant proclamations of the certainty of Christ's imminent return. For some, it even brings back memories of a tent with sawdust on the floor and beasts on the stage and a preacher exclaiming, "Soon! *Very* soon!"

But here we sit. And for some, here we *sleep.* So our question is, *How* do we wait? How do we watch? What does it mean to be wise? It means that even though we may at times grow tired and sleepy, we always maintain an experience with Christ in the soul. It is an experience fed by the Spirit and focused on a personal walk with Him. In fact, watching appropriately for the Bridegroom's arrival will have far less to do with how tired we have become, and will have everything to do with whether or not the oil of the Holy Spirit continues to move us forward in our personal walk with Jesus Christ. Why? Because watching has everything to do with who we know. *Watching means knowing Jesus in a personal, enduring way.*

---

[1] Craig S. Keener makes this point in *The IVP New Testament Commentary Series: Matthew* (Downers Grove, Ill.: Inter Varsity Press, 1997), 356.

[2] See Craig A. Evans and Stanley E. Porter, *Dictionary of New Testament Background* (Downers Grove, Ill.: Inter Varsity Press, 1997), 686.

[3] William Barclay, *The Daily Study Bible: The Gospel of Matthew,* revised edition (Philadelphia: Westminster Press, 1975), 2:319, 320.

[4] Ibid., 320.

CHAPTER SIX

One Sure Way to *Watch* Every Day

"Again, it will be like a man going on a journey, who called his servants and entrusted his property to them. To one he gave five talents of money, to another two talents, and to another one talent, each according to his ability. Then he went on his journey. The man who had received the five talents went at once and put his money to work and gained five more. So also, the one with the two talents gained two more. But the man who had received the one talent went off, dug a hole in the ground and hid his master's money.

"After a long time the master of those servants returned and settled accounts with them. The man who had received the five talents brought the other five. 'Master,' he said, 'you entrusted me with five talents. See, I have gained five more.'

"His master replied, 'Well done, good and faithful servant! You have been faithful with a few things; I will put you in charge of many things. Come and share your master's happiness!'

"The man with the two talents also came. 'Master,' he said, 'you entrusted me with two talents; see, I have gained two more.'

"His master replied, 'Well done, good and faithful servant! You have been faithful with a few things; I will put you in charge of many things. Come and share your master's happiness!'

"Then the man who had received the one talent came. 'Master,' he said, 'I knew that you are a hard man, harvesting where you have not sown and gathering where you have not scattered seed. So I was afraid and went out and hid your talent in the ground. See, here is what belongs to you.'

"His master replied, 'You wicked, lazy servant! So you knew that I harvest where I have not sown and gather where I have not scattered seed? Well then, you should have put my money on deposit with the bankers, so that when I returned I would have received it back with interest.

" 'Take the talent from him and give it to the one who has the ten talents. For everyone who has will be given more, and he will have an abundance. Whoever does not have, even what he has will be taken from him. And throw that worthless servant outside, into the darkness, where there will be weeping and gnashing of teeth' " (Matthew 25:14–30).

Some things look more ominous later than they do at the time. Americans have certainly discovered that since the events of September 11. There was a time when a group of men interested in flying lessons did not warrant a raised eyebrow. There was a time when a couple of men wanting to learn to fly crop dusters were forgotten in a few minutes. There was a time when I carried my little Swiss Army pocket-knife through airport security without a question. But no longer. Some things look more ominous later than they do at the time.

A *Newsweek* article, discussing some of the people who are being rounded up by law enforcement, points out how something that at the time may only seem curious can later seem threatening: "Federal law-enforcement officials estimate that there are perhaps a thousand people in the United States who have ties to terrorist organizations abroad. With cells in at least 60 countries, Al Qaeda has thousands more awaiting orders to strike. Rooting them out is going to be exceedingly difficult. *Clues are always clearer in hindsight.*"[1]

That last sentence catches my eye: *Clues are always clearer in hindsight.* Is that not just another way of saying, some things look more ominous later than they do at the time?

This well-known parable is like that. Most of us have read it many times, studied it in Bible study groups, and listened to more than a few sermons preached on it. It has become, in fact, so much a part of our common life and language that a central element in the parable—the talent—has developed its own meaning, quite separate from the meaning it had at the time the story was told. When it was first told a talent referred to a unit of exchange; but because of this story, in the Middle Ages the word *talent* came to mean a God-given ability or gift. [2]

And yet, consider this: When Christians met together a couple of years ago to talk about the coming of Christ, had they discussed how to prepare for His advent, chances are that among all of the tasks and duties and themes that might have been raised, most would never have even have thought of this parable.

After all, is it not just another story? An important story, certainly, but just a story where Jesus recommends that we use our talents, that we develop our gifts and abilities. Nothing too serious about that.

But then we realize that *the end of time is here. Again.* So we turn to the two chapters where Christ speaks His clearest words regarding His coming and, right at the heart of what He has to say, we find this parable. And it is then that the truly serious, urgent nature of the story emerges.

What does it mean to watch for the coming of Christ? has been our question in the last two chapters and is our question again in this chapter. We again sit at Jesus' feet, listening as He tells us a third story. He begins by saying, "Again, it will be like . . . " The "it" to which Jesus here refers is the kingdom of heaven specifically displayed in His coming a second time. So we again press home to Him the question, "Jesus, how do we wait and watch for Your coming?"

The parable says that the master gives talents to his servants. It does not explicitly say *why* he gave them, but a similar parable in Luke 19 suggests that the master gives his servants talents for two reasons: One, for them to use in such a way as to increase the master's holdings; and two, to see if they would use them in a way that would give evidence of their reliability and faithfulness. And so he gives them talents—to one he gives five, to another he gives two, and to the last one he gives one. Each one receives according to the ability that he has manifested in the past.

Remember, a talent *then* was not a talent as we use the word *now*. In that day and time a talent was simply a unit of exchange, a weight measurement. The value of the talent depended on what was being weighed. If gold or silver or copper was being weighed, the value of a talent would vary according to the price of the metal. One thing is certain, however: The talents distributed by the master represented something far more valuable than these servants would ever have been able to earn on their own.[3]

For our purposes in understanding the parable, a talent might represent any gift given to us by God, whether that is a responsibility He has given us, an ability with which we were born, or a faculty we have developed.

The story starts well and ends badly, and there is one simple reason for this: The third servant never did put his talent to use. I wonder why? If he had it, why did he not use it?

Maybe he was like we have often been: He simply did not realize the seriousness with which he should treat this talent; he did not realize the implications at stake for not putting it to use. He thought it was just another choice in life with no particularly significant consequences. He did not realize that what he did with the talent had everything to do with *watching* for the master's return. We noted earlier: Some things look more ominous later than they did at the time. And maybe that's what happened to the servant. Maybe that is why he did not put his talent to use.

Or maybe he did not put it to use because he felt inadequate. After all, the other two servants had more talents than he did. "So let them do it."

I took voice lessons in college. Those who know me will doubtless be quite surprised. After about a year of lessons, I gave up, and the teacher changed careers. That's not a joke! I think he may have wanted to do something more promising. But while I was taking lessons, he required me to do something that he required of all of his voice students: sing a solo at church. At the *big* college church!

It just so happened that the Friday night he selected for me to sing was a weekend when the Heritage Singers were in town. Now, they were not singing at that meeting, but the news of their coming concert left a certain expectation in the air. And I was supposed to sing for vespers! *Please!*

Let me tell you—I begged and pleaded and coaxed and promised, but he refused to budge. "You *have* to do it," he said. "We'll pick a good song."

So I sang, "I Walked Today Where Jesus Walked." I think that song covers about nineteen octaves.

How did it go? you ask. Well, let me remind you: The teacher changed careers, and I have never been asked to sing again!

I do not ever remember feeling more inadequate, more untalented, and more incompetent than I did when I quaked up to that pulpit and croaked out that song. "So, servant, you of the one talent, I understand. When everyone else is so talented, what am *I* doing up here? Let someone *else* use his or her talent. They are much better at it than I am."

So maybe that's why he buried his talent. He just felt small. The others had more than he did. *They* could do the job.

Not realizing the seriousness of the task or knowing that others have more talents than I do are good excuses for not doing something, but they are not the reasons the Bible gives for the servant's choice. The Bible gives a different, but simpler reason. It is contained in three words in verse 25: "I was afraid." And that explains everything, because fear paralyzes action.

A couple of years ago, a good friend and I scaled Half Dome at Yosemite National Park. While there, I watched an interesting occurrence. We were at the top of the dome on a cloudy day. The clouds had by and large socked in the mountain, and we could not see the valley floor. Regardless, I stayed away from that sheer precipice of two or three thousand feet. But I did watch a young man get very close to the edge. While I was standing there, fifteen or twenty feet from the edge, this young man confidently sauntered up to the edge and sat down with his feet hanging over the precipice. Now remember, *this is a sheer drop of two or three thousand feet.* And he sat there with his feet dangling over the edge!

I stood there watching him, wondering exactly who had let him out of whatever institution he had been in! And then suddenly, the clouds parted. It did not last long, just a few seconds. But for those few brief seconds we could see all the way to the valley floor. I cannot quite name the sound that I heard come from this young man, but I can mimic it. It sounded something like: *"Ooohhhhhhohhoh."* His back went rigid, and he slowly and gingerly inched back from the precipice.

Fear paralyzes action.

During his years as premier of the Soviet Union, Nikita Khrushchev denounced many of the policies and atrocities of his predecessor, Joseph Stalin. One day, in a public meeting, he censured

Stalin for some of what he had done. Suddenly a heckler from the audience shouted out: "You were a comrade to Stalin. Why didn't you stop him?"

"Who said that?" roared Khrushchev. An agonizing silence descended upon the room. No one spoke. No one dared move a muscle. And then, after several seconds of tense silence, Khrushchev replied quietly, "*Now* you know why I didn't try to stop him."[4]

Make no mistake about it: Fear paralyzes action. Maybe that recognition is what led Max Lucado to write these words: "Fear doesn't want you to make the journey to the mountain. If he can rattle you enough, fear will persuade you to take your eyes off the peaks and settle for a dull existence in the flatlands."[5]

Since fear does that to us, and since it did that to the third servant, the next words in verse 25 make absolute sense: "I was afraid," so I "went . . . and hid." Absolutely understandable, is it not? The servant was dominated by fear, so when he was finally able to act, he hid. He hid his talent in the safest hiding place of the day—the ground.

I wonder how often that little scenario is played out in the church. "I was afraid, so I went and hid." There are good hiding places. You can hide behind more talented people, bigger, more important people, people who seem to be more righteous. You can hide in the back of the sanctuary, on the fringes of the group, in the middle of the crowd. There are all kinds of hiding places. Places where others will never find you.

But there is One who *will* notice, because this parable is not about how much the church needs you and your gifts, though it most certainly does. This parable is about how to live in readiness for the coming of the Master. And the servant soon discovers that he cannot hide from the master.

The master returned. And notice that, *unlike* the last two parables, there is no surprise noted, but *like* the last two parables, once again the master was a long time in coming (see verse 19). And when he finally returns, he calls for an accounting. The third servant is not ready. Why is he not ready? Because he has done nothing with his talent. He was afraid of the master, afraid the master was too demanding, so he buried it. And he reaps a grim sentence.

A letter was published some years ago in *USA Today* (September 17, 1990) written to pop singer George Michael. It seems that in a previous article, George Michael had said he wanted to back away from all the celebrity and fame his singing career had brought him. One reader was so disturbed by Michael's decision that he wrote a letter to him. Here are some excerpts from the letter:

> I don't understand a guy who lives "in hopes of reducing the strain of his celebrity status." Come on, George. Loosen up. Swing, man. Dust off those gossamer wings and fly yourself to the moon of your choice and be grateful to carry the baggage we've all had to carry since those lean nights of sleeping on buses and helping unload the instruments.
>
> And no more of that talk about "the tragedy of fame." The tragedy of fame is when no one shows up and you're singing to the cleaning lady in some empty joint that hasn't seen a paying customer [in ages].

Then the writer added one last piece of advice:

> Talent must not be wasted. Those who have it—and you obviously do or the article would have been about [someone else] . . . must hug it, embrace it, nurture it and share it lest it be taken away from you as fast as it was loaned to you.
>
> Trust me. I've been there.

It was signed:

Frank Sinatra, Rancho Mirage.

Well, I never thought I'd quote such an ultimate source of truth as Frank Sinatra, but I must say, the man has a point. Did you notice what he said? "Talent must not be wasted. Those who have it . . . must hug it, embrace it, nurture it and share it lest it be taken away . . . as fast as it was loaned." Does that sound vaguely familiar to the reader of the Gospel of Matthew?

Sinatra is right. The talent was taken away from the servant as quickly as it was loaned to him. And the third servant's story ends tragically. He was not watching for the return of the master, and he was caught unprepared.

Fortunately, there are two other servants for whom the parable has a joyous ending. *They* are ready! *They* greet their master with joy! And his ringing affirmation to them of a job well done echoes all the way down to our time.

Why are these first two servants ready? The answer to *that* is the answer to our question of how we are to watch. The first two servants realized that their ability to look their master in the eye at his return would depend on whether or not they had used his gifts to increase his holdings. Simply stated, watching means using your talents to increase the kingdom of God.

Have you thought about what that means?

First of all, take it for what it literally meant to the first hearers, when a talent symbolized money. So one of the first ways to watch is using your money in ways that further the goals of the kingdom of God.

Have you ever realized that when the offering plate comes down your row at church and you drop in your tithe and your offerings that you are not just giving to the church? No, you are *watching,* watching for the coming of Christ. Have you ever realized that when the hat is passed for a needy family and you help bear the burden, you are not just giving something to help the needy? No, you are *watching* for the coming.

But we must also appropriately broaden the meaning of the talent to include not only money, but to also include the responsibilities, gifts, talents, and abilities that God gives to each one of us. And when we do that, we realize that every day of our lives can be characterized by watching.

When outstanding musicians lead worshipers in majestic praise; when the choir and orchestra use what they have been given to lift the hearts of God's people heavenward, it is tempting just to say, "Thank you for using your talents." And that is fine, as far as it goes. But please understand that on a much deeper level, as they increase the kingdom of God, they are *watching.* Watching for the coming.

When children learn of the truths of the kingdom in children's programs, they are the beneficiaries of people who are using their talents to increase the kingdom in their little lives. And so we say, "Thank you for using your talents." But, beyond that, do not miss the fact that these leaders are not just serving the children. No. They are *watching*. Watching for the coming of the King. Drama groups who help to illustrate the truths of the kingdom are not just entertainment. They are using their talents to increase an understanding of the kingdom. That is *watching*.

When physicians and nurses and other healthcare professionals use the gifts they have been given to alleviate suffering, we are thankful when health is restored. We thank them for a job well done. We are grateful that they are working in the tradition of the Great Physician to address the physical needs of people. But we must also remember, they are *watching*.

And we could name so many others who are faithfully using their talents in ways that enlarge the kingdom of God. Everywhere you look, every day of your life, when you see faithful servants of Christ putting to use their talents to increase the kingdom, thank them, appreciate them, be grateful to them, and then realize that they are only doing what we must all do if we are to live in readiness for the coming. *They are watching.* They are watching every day in a way that we never outgrow.

When Jimmy Carter, the thirty-ninth president of the United States, left the White House in 1981, he did not retire to a life of ease. Carter is a committed Christian and a longtime Sunday School teacher. So when he was through with the most visible job in the world, he went to work with Habitat for Humanity and busied himself in many diplomatic peacekeeping missions.

Carter said in the *New Yorker:*

> When Rosalynn and I left the White House, we decided since I was one of the youngest survivors of the office and we had a lot of years ahead of us, and I was deeply interested in human rights, and I didn't want to just build a library and go back to farming—we would do things that others wouldn't or couldn't do.
>
> To me, this is part of my duty as a human being. It is part of my duty to capitalize on my reputation and fame and influence as a former President of a great nation. And it's exciting. It's unpredictable. It's gratifying. It's adventurous. I just enjoy it.[6]

When we use our talents in such ways, the Master will return with a smile on His face and say, "Well done! Come into My joy!"

The third servant had accused the master of being a hard man. And landowners at that time probably *were* hard men. But in this parable Jesus is using this contrast: If the motivation to work for a harsh man is strong, *how much more* motivated should we be who work for a God of whom we do not have to be afraid?

Some years ago I watched a TV news program about Billy Graham. The interviewer asked Graham about his life, his ministry, and his family. It was a touching piece on the life of a man who had dedicated himself to using any talent he has to increasing the kingdom of God. Toward the end of the story the interviewer asked him a question that caught my attention: "Looking back over a life well lived, what is left? What do you desire most?"

Graham thought about that for a moment, and then looking the interviewer in the eye, in a voice tinged with emotion, he said: "What I desire most of all is to one day hear my Lord speak the words, 'Well done, good and faithful servant. Enter into My joy.' "

Do you yearn, along with Billy Graham, to hear those words? Do you long to live in such a way as to be always ready? Then let me give you one sure way to watch every day. Put your talents—whatever they are—to use in increasing the kingdom of God, and you will be watching. Because *watching means using your talents to increase His kingdom.*

[1] *Newsweek,* October 29, 2001, 44. Italics mine.

[2] See *The New Interpreter's Bible* (Nashville: Abingdon Press, 1995), 8:453.

[3] Michael Green, *The Message of Matthew* (Downers Grove, Ill.: InterVarsity Press, 2000), 261; and William Barclay, *The Daily Study Bible: The Gospel of Matthew,* revised edition (Philadelphia: Westminster Press, 1975), 2:322.

[4] *Today in the Word,* July 13, 1993, found in http://www.sermonillustrations.com/a-z/f/fear.htm, November 1, 2002.

[5] Max Lucado, *Tomorrow's Dream, Today's Courage* (Word, 1991), 11.

[6] From Craig Brian Larson, *Choice Contemporary Stories and Illustrations for Preachers, Teachers and Writers* (Grand Rapids, Mich.: Baker Books, 1998), 73.

CHAPTER SEVEN

The Bottom Line

Back in the mid-1980s, someone in Hollywood made an entirely forgettable movie named *Volunteers*. In the movie, Tom Hanks stars as a rich kid named Lawrence who has a large debt. His father refuses to help pay off his debt, so Lawrence joins the Peace Corps and escapes on a flight to Southeast Asia. There his assignment is to help build a bridge for the local villagers. What the Peace Corps workers do not realize is that the U.S. Army, a local Communist force, and a powerful drug lord all covet the bridge. Together with the help of the only English-speaking native, they must fight off the three opposing forces and find out what is right for the villagers, as well as for themselves.[1]

I have long since forgotten just about everything about the movie, with one exception. Lawrence, the rich kid with the big debt, makes a comment about the needy people around him. Noting their need, he says, "It's not that I *can't* help these people; it's that I don't *want* to."

Lyndon Johnson expressed that same attitude in the early 1960s. In a statement reflecting such a spirit, he said to Americans, "Don't forget, there are two hundred million of us in a world of three billion. They want what we've got—and we're not going to give it to them."[2]

What do these two statements, made by such disparate people as Lyndon Johnson and a character played by Tom Hanks, have to do with this book? In previous chapters, we have been asking, "*How* do we watch for the coming of Christ? What does Jesus mean when He tells us to *watch*?"

We are in a section in Matthew's Gospel where Jesus is preaching parables and prophecy. It is a passage filled with hope and help for us as we contemplate the coming. The passage finds its roots in the words, " 'O Jerusalem, Jerusalem . . . how often I have longed to gather your children together, as a hen gathers her chicks under her wings, but you were not willing' " (Matthew 23:37). Here Jesus speaks His most explicit words regarding His coming and the end of the world.

We have listened to Jesus speak and we have learned much about how to live a life of readiness. But as we approach this last part of the passage, we do so with a question burning in our minds: Just what is "the bottom line"? What is the rest of story?

If it is true that good speakers save the punch line for the end, then we can expect that in this passage Jesus will speak plainly, passionately, poignantly. This is His final parable in His final discourse in Matthew. After these words, Matthew's story of Jesus turns to the final episodes of His life. These are His last sermonic words. So we can imagine that now as Jesus speaks of readiness for His coming, He will speak clearly of what will ultimately be the dividing line between the saved and the lost. And when He does so, He will speak in ways so simple that it is impossible for us to misunderstand.

This passage is technically *not* a parable, though it does have certain elements of a parable.[3] It speaks of a shepherd, of sheep and goats, and of a separation between the two. But it is actually an apocalyptic drama. In broad, vivid strokes Jesus paints a penetrating portrait of what in the judgment will constitute readiness.

One element is consistently clear in each of the parables we have considered: Though it takes a long time—far longer than anyone would have expected—in every case, in each parable, the story ends with the return of the master or the bridegroom. In other words, *he will come.* Though he delays, *he will return.*

The first truth of the parable is a truly stunning one: *Christ is the Judge.* He sits there a wearied man. The sands in the hourglass of His life are running very low. The limited nature of His life has never been keener. And this dusty, travel-worn Teacher sits there with the valley of Jehoshaphat at His feet. Every good Jew considered this valley to be the scene of final judgment. And the lowly Nazarene gazes on that scene, and with eye undimmed and in language so unlimited in its claims that the Speaker must either be a madman or God Himself, He lays claim to being the Judge of all the earth. All else that He says in this parable is intended to tune us into exactly what it means to watch as we prepare for that juncture with judgment.

Shepherds often separated sheep and goats at night. Sheep were the more valuable of the two, they tolerated cool air much better, and they were usually associated with good things. Goats, on the other hand, were less valuable, needed to huddle together for warmth, and were usually associated with trouble. At night, then, shepherds often separated the sheep from the goats. Christ's parable deals with this separation, and does so against the backdrop of the end of the world.

"When the Son of Man comes in his glory, and all the angels with him, he will sit on his throne in heavenly glory. All the nations will be gathered before him, and he will separate the people one from another as a shepherd separates the sheep from the goats. He will put the sheep on his right and the goats on his left.

"Then the King will say to those on his right, 'Come, you who are blessed by my Father; take your inheritance, the kingdom prepared for you since the creation of the world. For I was hungry and you gave me something to eat, I was thirsty and you gave me something to drink, I was a stranger and you invited me in, I needed clothes and you clothed me, I was sick and you looked after me, I was in prison and you came to visit me.'

"Then the righteous will answer him, 'Lord, when did we see you hungry and feed you, or thirsty and give you something to drink? When did we see you a stranger and invite you in, or needing clothes and clothe you? When did we see you sick or in prison and go to visit you?'

"The King will reply, 'I tell you the truth, whatever you did for one of the least of these brothers of mine, you did for me.'

"Then he will say to those on his left, 'Depart from me, you who are cursed, into the eternal fire prepared for the devil and his angels. For I was hungry and you gave me nothing to eat, I was thirsty and you gave me nothing to drink, I was a stranger and you did not invite me in, I needed clothes and you did not clothe me, I was sick and in prison and you did not look after me.'

"They also will answer, 'Lord, when did we see you hungry or thirsty or a stranger or needing clothes or sick or in prison, and did not help you?'

"He will reply, 'I tell you the truth, whatever you did not do for one of the least of these, you did not do for me.'

"Then they will go away to eternal punishment, but the righteous to eternal life" (Matthew 25:31–46).

One theologian suggests that this parable not only says that the Son of Man *will come;* but also says that the Son of Man has come *already,* but that He has come in disguise. Both His first and second comings are public and open, but in between, people are blind to the Christ who joins us and who judges us by our reaction to the poor and needy.[4]

Please notice three surprises in the parable.

First of all, notice the surprise of the lost. The discovery that they have at some point in their lives encountered Jesus elicits a response of legitimate surprise, a significant shock, an unsettling jolt of reality. "What do You mean, we are being judged based on how we treated You? We've never even *seen* You! Or if we did, we certainly didn't *recognize* You. In fact, if we *did* see You, if we had only known it was You, we most certainly would have done things differently. We would have helped You." (See Matthew 25:34–46.) They are frankly surprised at this discovery. If they had recognized Jesus, their responses would have been very different.

While I was in college, my brother and sister and I lived in a house several miles out in the country. Late one night I was driving home from the campus. I remember the night, misty and cold and wet, not a good night to be out. And yet, as I drove down the country highway I sped past a man jogging beside the road. *What in the world is somebody doing out jogging at this hour on a night like this? That's awfully strange!* I thought. *Oh well, to each his own.*

I had been home about thirty minutes when my brother came in the front door. He was hot and sweaty and tired . . . and upset!

"Man, my car breaks down five miles down the road, and you go *whizzing* past me and don't even slow down! What's the deal?"

"John! I didn't know that was you! I had no idea. If I had *known* it was you, I certainly would have stopped! I just thought it was someone out jogging!"

Familiar words, laced with surprise: "Lord, if we had known that was *You*, we would've done something. We thought it was just some common person."

In his book, *Rebuild Your Life*, Dale Galloway tells a story worth noting. Years ago, a young man returned from fighting in the Vietnam War. He arrived in California. When he did so, he placed a phone call home to his parents in Boston. His parents were high-society Bostonians. They relished the cocktail-circuit party crowd and everything that went with it.

The young man called home and his mother answered the phone.

"Mom," he said, "I just called to tell you that I want to bring a war buddy home with me."

His mother said, "OK, well, bring him along for a few days."

"But, Mother," said the young man, "there is something you need to know about him. He was very badly injured in the war. He was caught in an explosion during a battle, and one leg and one arm were blown off, one eye is gone, and his face is quite disfigured. Is it still all right with you if I bring him home?"

His mother said, "Well, I guess so. Bring him home for a few days."

The son said, "You don't understand me, Mother. I want to bring him home to *live* with us."

The mother began to make excuses. "I don't know," she said. "Someone like that is going to feel embarrassed around our friends. And what would people think?" and she was going on and on when the phone clicked. Her son had hung up on her.

Not too many hours later the California police called that high-society Boston home. Once again, the mother answered. After introductions, the police sergeant at the other end of the line said, "We just found a young man with one arm, one leg, one eye and a mangled face. He just committed suicide. His identification papers say he is your son."[5]

One wonders, would it have made a difference . . . would the conversation have reached a different conclusion . . . would the young man's life have had a different end, had she known that *he* was the mangled veteran? In terms of the parable, it does not really matter: Jesus says that we are judged based on our response to *Him*, and since *He* is disguised in the appearance of human need, our response to the needs around us reveals the true attitude of our heart.

Thus, for those on the left, the true attitude of the heart was that *they did not care.* So the first surprise we notice is the surprise of the lost: "We didn't know that was You! If we had known it was You, we would have done something."

But there's a second surprise in the parable: the surprise of the saved. And their surprise is remarkably similar to the surprise of the lost. They, too, are surprised that they have seen Jesus. In fact, their words are remarkably similar to the words of the lost. "What do You mean, we are being judged based on how we treated You? We've never even *seen* You! Or if we did, we certainly didn't recognize You. When did we see You and help You?"

But the key element in their surprise is this: Knowing or not knowing who it was that they were helping *would not have changed their behavior.* In this, they are very different from the lost. They would still have done the same things. Their response reveals their heart. It probes exactly why it was that they did these things. And why did they do them? They did them simply because they cared.

A student once asked anthropologist Margaret Mead for the earliest sign of civilization in a given culture. He perhaps expected her answer to be that it was a clay pot or a fishhook or a grinding stone. Mead said, the earliest sign of civilization in a given culture was a healed femur—a broken leg that had healed. Why? No mended bones are found where the law of the jungle—survival of the fittest—reigns. But a healed femur shows that someone cared. Someone had to do the injured person's hunting and gathering until the leg healed. Someone had to take care of the person until she had mended sufficiently to be able to once again begin to fend for herself. So, said Mead, the evidence of compassion is the first sign of civilization.[6]

Drawing together what the other three parables say about watching with what this parable says is instructive. It suggests that people who are watching in *those* ways—the ways suggested by the other parables—*care* about the human needs around them.

What does such caring cause them to do? Well, the acts that Jesus here lists are mostly standard acts of Jewish piety. But please notice two things about them. First, of all, notice that these deeds are *simple* deeds. Someone is hungry and needs food; someone else is thirsty and needs water; a person is a stranger and needs a friend; someone else is naked and in need of clothes; a woman is sick and in need of care; a man is in prison and in need of visitors. These are simple needs with simple solutions. There is nothing mentioned here that is outside the reach of any one of us. There are no dramatic acts here recorded—no miracles, no marvelous acts, no outstanding events. Just caring for the simple needs of needy people.

But these deeds are not only simple; they meet *basic* needs, necessary for survival. These are bottom-line needs. They remind us of the lower levels of Maslow's hierarchy of needs. Jesus is here talking about the kinds of things that people need in order to survive. He is not saying that caring for these needs means that we have to donate large sums of money to charity or that we have to travel long distances to preach the gospel or that we have to establish organizations to change the world or anything of the sort. No. He is simply saying that the basic needs of the people around us give us the opportunity to show Jesus how much we care about *Him.* Furthermore, Jesus says that on the last day, our commendation or our condemnation depends on whether or not we have done precisely that. Simply put, *watching means caring,* caring for the simple and basic needs of others.

Forgive me for feeling some familial pride, and forgive me furthermore for telling this story without the permission of the gentleman involved. Years ago, a woman in South America came to Christ because of something she witnessed. It happened on a busy street corner. A crippled beggar woman sat on the curb waiting for the busy flow of cars to allow her to push herself across the intersection on her makeshift skateboard-like transportation. But the cars would not stop coming. A rather well-to-do woman in a nearby building watched from a window as the minutes passed with no hope of the beggar woman crossing the street. Then, she would later say, along came a tall American gentleman. He paused at the street corner, also waiting. Then he bent down and briefly conversed with the handicapped woman. A moment later he stooped down, gathered her up in his arms, and carried her across the street. Reaching the other side, he gently set her down and then continued on his way.

Watching from the window, the well-to-do woman saw what happened and said, "I must find out who that man is and what he does." She found that he was a pastor, and she ultimately joined his church. She also found out his name. Most people call him Pastor; I just call him Dad. Later, he had to struggle to remember the incident.

Maybe the most poignant touch of the parable is the surprise of the righteous. They thought they were just caring for common people, ordinary people, people who are all too easily and all too soon forgotten. And yet, Christ says, "That was *Me* you carried across the street. When you stooped down and picked her up, you did that for Me."

In 1921, Lewis Lawes became the warden of Sing Sing Prison. During that time, no prison was tougher than Sing Sing. But by the time Warden Lawes retired some twenty years later, the prison had become a much more humanitarian institution. Those who studied the system said the credit for the change belonged to Lawes. But when he was asked about the transformation, he said simply, "I owe it all to my wonderful wife, Catherine."

When Lawes became the warden, Catherine was a young mother with three small children. Here they were, within the reach of one of the most dreaded prisons of the day. Everybody warned her from the beginning that she should never set foot inside the prison walls. But Catherine decided otherwise. She would become a part of the life of those who were imprisoned. Her attitude was: "My husband and I are going to take care of these men, and I believe they will take care of us! I don't have to worry!"

When the first prison basketball game was held, she walked into the gym with her three beautiful kids and actually sat in the stands with the inmates. She insisted on getting acquainted with them and their records. She discovered that one convicted murderer was blind, so she paid him a visit. Holding his hand in hers, she asked, "Do you read Braille?"

"What's Braille?" he asked.

Over a period of time she answered his question by teaching him how to read.

Some time later, Catherine found a deaf prisoner. She went to school and learned how to use sign language in order to communicate with him. Many prisoners and others said that Catherine Lawes was the body of Jesus that came alive again in Sing Sing from 1921 to 1937.

Then, tragedy struck. Catherine Lawes was killed in an automobile accident. The morning after her death, Lewis Lawes did not come to work, so the second in command took his place. It seemed that almost instantly the entire prison population knew what had happened. The prisoners were grief-stricken.

The following day, her body was placed in a casket in her home, three-quarters of a mile from the prison. As the second in command took his early morning walk, he was shocked to see a large crowd of the toughest, hardest looking prisoners imaginable gathered in front of the main gate. He came closer and saw tears of grief and sadness. He knew how much they had loved Catherine. After thinking for a moment, he turned and faced the men and made an unprecedented concession. "All right, men, you can go. You can go see her. You can go pay your respects. But you must check back in immediately afterwards!" He then opened the gate and a parade of prisoners walked, without a guard, the three-quarters of a mile to the Lawes home to stand in line to pay their final respects to Catherine. When their time was over, and when it was time to check the prison count, every single prisoner had checked back in. *Every single one!*[7]

But that may not be the most arresting part of the story. Maybe the most surprising part is yet to come. It will happen one day when we see a young warden's wife stand before the judgment bar of God. God's soul-searching eyes scan her face. He reads her very soul. And then a smile twinkles in His eyes. "Come in, Catherine!" He says. "Come in. I welcome you here because you welcomed Me there. The door to My kingdom is open wide for you because of the way you treated Me."

"But, Lord," says a surprised young mother, "I don't understand. I've never even seen You!"

"Oh, yes," He says. "Yes, you have. Your gracious hands once clutched Mine as together our fingers brushed across bumpy pages learning to read Braille. Your benevolent hands once expressed words of comfort and courage to My eyes, because My ears could not hear.

"You see, Catherine, you thought those were just prisoners. But those weren't just prisoners. *I* was there in that prison, in the person of needy prisoners longing to be touched by the love of God. And you did that for Me."

And a surprised young mother enters the kingdom.

The parable has three surprises, and we've noticed two. The first two surprises in the parable are the surprise of the lost and the surprise of the saved. And both have to do with not realizing that they have seen Jesus. "We didn't know it was You!" is their exclamation of astonishment.

But there is one more surprise. Only this surprise is ours! Oh, this may also have surprised the original hearers of the parable, but it is particularly surprising to *us*. And the surprise is this: We might have expected that when it came to the bottom line,

Jesus would have said something different. We might have expected that once He had laid out in the first three parables the broad strokes of how to watch for His coming, now that He was coming to the last word, He would have emphasized the specific details of the events that would precede His coming. Or that He would speak with us of theology or righteousness or obedience. Or that He would call us to an open confession of our faith in Him. Or that He would speak of grace and justification and forgiveness.

But He does none of these. When it comes to the bottom line, Jesus basically asks us the question, "Are you serious enough about your faith, about your profession, about your claims to My name, that you will take all of your theology, all of your beliefs, all of your ethics, and wrap them up in a package that will respond to human need?" In other words, *Do you care?* Do you care enough about others to go about meeting their simple and basic needs? Because *watching means caring for the simple and basic needs of others.*

---

[1] I drew some of the summary of this movie from a summary written by Michael Silva at http://us.imdb.com/Plot?0090274, November 1, 2002.

[2] Quoted in Michael Hodgin, *1001 More Humorous Illustrations for Public Speaking.* (Grand Rapids, Mich.: Zondervan, 1998), 337.

[3] D. A. Carson, *The Expositor's Bible Commentary* (Grand Rapids, Mich.: Zondervan, 1984), 8:518.

[4] Michael Green, *The Message of Matthew* (Downers Grove, Ill.: InterVarsity Press, 2000), 263, 264.

[5] Dale E. Galloway, *Rebuild Your Life,* quoted in Charles R. Swindoll, *The Tale of the Tardy Oxcart* (Nashville: Word, 1998), 109.

[6] R. Wayne Willis, quoted in Edward K. Rowell, *Fresh Illustrations for Preaching and Teaching* (Grand Rapids: Baker Books, 1997), 22.

[7] I have used this story almost exactly in the form I found it at http://www.sermoncentral.com/sercentral/sermon.asp?SermonID=34912&ContributorID=5921, November 1, 2002.

CHAPTER EIGHT

Now What?

Since the end of time is here again, we have journeyed with Jesus over the terrain of events and teachings about the last things. We began our journey by eavesdropping on the disciples of old as they asked Jesus questions: "Lord, *'When?'* and *'What?'* When will You return and *what* will be the sign of Your return?" We overheard as Jesus refocused them (and us) onto *who?* and *how?*

"Who is it whom we await? Who is the One who will return?" It is our Lord who will come, our Master, our Savior, and our Friend.

And *"How? How* do we watch for His coming? What does it mean to watch?"

Jesus has been clear and simple in His answers:

Watching means doing, doing the Master's bidding.
Watching means knowing, knowing Jesus on a personal, enduring basis.

Watching means using, using our talents to increase His kingdom.

And *watching means caring,* caring for the simple and basic needs of others.

Now what? Now that we know these things, what difference do they make? What do we do now? What does all of this mean for the way in which we live life day in and day out? What are the implications of understanding preparation for the coming in this way? Are there any final take-home lessons for us as we leave the last conversation (in the book of Matthew) that Jesus will have with His disciples before the final events of His life unfold?

Five lessons will be helpful in translating what Jesus said *then* into our everyday lives *now.*

First of all, we must remember that *what seems lasting really isn't.* Upon leaving the temple with Jesus that day, His disciples pointed out its magnificence to Him. Doubtless, it was a splendid sight! The temple occupied the center of both Jewish hope and Jewish pride. It symbolized the permanence of the nation and its dreams for the future. Even while the *Pax Romana* dominated the world, the temple still stood for all that they were and hoped to be. It must have seemed as enduring to them as their hopes and dreams for their nation's future.

And yet Jesus' response to His disciples was, "Do you see all these buildings? The time is coming when not one stone will be left upon another. All will be thrown down." We could update His words by paraphrasing them this way: "Be careful—for what seems to be lasting really isn't."

As I wrote these words on my laptop computer, our family was on a flight out of the Newark, New Jersey, airport. The day before, we spent most of the day in lower Manhattan. While there, we spent several hours at Ground Zero. Hovering constantly in my thoughts was a day more than twenty years ago when a friend and I, on a summer vacation trip from seminary, walked the same streets. We entered the South Tower of the World Trade Center and rode the express elevator to the top. Standing on the observation deck, we took in the incredible vistas of New York harbor. From that distance, Lady Liberty was a toy, the Empire State Building was a second-class citizen, and, on a clear day with strong binoculars, you could see forever (almost!).

The possibility of these buildings collapsing never even crossed my mind. In fact, had you asked me that day about their permanence—"Do you think these towers will last?"—I could have answered unequivocally: "Absolutely." I would have said, "These towers are one of the marvels of modern-day engineering. They are solid, stable, *lasting.*"

Yesterday, from the World Trade Center Viewing Site on Liberty Street, we gazed down into a mammoth hole. The large trucks and cranes below looked like toys. They were hard at work rebuilding the train station that had been below the ground in the belly of the World Trade Center. The authorities apparently wish to finish the train station first in order to restore subway service. Then, once the final decision is made regarding what will replace the Twin Towers, a strengthened train station will already be in place.

Gazing into that enormous hole, I wondered, *How can they be gone? Just gone? They were so big, so beautiful, so lasting.* But they did not last. Now they exist only in our pictures and in our memories. And the effects of their collapse—on levels economic, political, social, and emotional—will continue to be felt for many years to come.

Jesus warned His disciples of the same thing. "Be careful where you put your trust, for the things that appear to last, will not." This lesson has important implications for us. It is a reminder that despite the fact that we hoped that Jesus would have come ere now, the fact that He has not must not lull us into thinking that all things will forever continue as they now are. It is tempting to think that since it has not happened yet, our lives will continue to go on as they always have. We will continue to work, play, invest our money, enjoy our friends, and live the life we always have. Nothing will change. All these things will last. And last . . .

Remember Christ's words a bit later in Matthew 24? "As it was in the days of Noah, so it will be at the coming of the Son of Man. For in the days before the flood, people were eating and drinking, marrying and giving in marriage, up to the day Noah entered the ark; and they knew nothing about what would happen until the flood came and took them all away. That is how it will be at the coming of the Son of Man" (verses 37–39). Life as usual was going on. Everything seemed lasting. Things would never change. And it was in the very ordinary-ness of life that it came to a shattering culmination. Jesus reminds His disciples to learn from that. "What seems lasting, really isn't."

About four decades after Christ spoke these words they were fulfilled. Jerusalem and that beautiful, seemingly lasting temple were destroyed. Those still living who remembered what He had said experienced first-hand the full impact of His prophecy—*what seems lasting, really isn't.*

Since that is true, there are important implications regarding how we live in light of the coming. There are questions we need to answer: What matters most to us in life? Where will we make the major investments of our time, talents, and treasures? Besides the necessities of daily living, are we making investments in things that will *last,* such as relationships, people, and the spiritual life? Where do we place our trust?

Another lesson follows hard on the heels of this one. Having said that the things which appear to be lasting really aren't, Jesus hastens to tell His disciples that the situation in the world *will get a great deal worse before it gets immeasurably better.*

In 1993 the basement immediately next to the North Tower of the World Trade Center was bombed. It withstood the bombing, as most Americans, and all New Yorkers in particular, remember. We were told that the terrorists who had attempted to destroy it might have been trying to topple it into the South Tower and thus bring both of them down. *Impossible,* I thought. *Inconceivable. Such a thing could never happen. The destruction would be of cataclysmic proportions.* Despite the sorrowful success of terrorism over the years and around the world, it was unimaginable to think that a small group of men could actually do something worse than blow up a bus or bring down an airliner. But then came September 11, 2001. And this time around, the result was disastrously worse than the first.

Jesus tells His disciples of one certainty about their future as followers of His: *It will get a great deal worse before it gets immeasurably better.* "For then there will be great distress, unequaled from the beginning of the world until now—and never to be equaled again" (Matthew 24:21). There is some scholarly debate over exactly which period of history Jesus refers to here. If, however, we view these words in the light of the catastrophic descriptions of Revelation, we can be quite certain that even now, two millennia after Christ first uttered the words, they are still true—it will *still* get much worse before the coming.

When I was a college student, we students would sometimes do community surveys asking people of their beliefs and understanding about God, the Bible, and life. Our hope was to not only understand the community better, but to ultimately be able to study the Bible with the people we interviewed. One of the survey questions was, "Do you think that the world is getting better or is it getting worse?"

I was surprised by the high percentage of people answering that question by affirming a rather strong belief that things would indeed get better. In their view, the future looked brighter than the present. Humankind was continuing to improve its condition with new inventions that would make life easier and better. Brighter days were ahead!

I wonder what the same people would say today. In light of the events of the past twenty years, it seems that all but the most incurably optimistic would say that, in fact, the future actually looks dark. Perusing the daily headlines is sufficient to convince one of that. Maybe that is why psychiatrists and psychologists tell us that the maladies that they treat most commonly are anxiety-related. The political landscape, international relations, the environment, not to speak of the looming threat of terrorism, have deeply scarred our psyche. We are scared! I have wondered if the T-shirt and bumper sticker slogan, "No Fear!" isn't just one more way of appearing to stave off the panic.

Jesus would understand all of this. In fact, He warned that as history moves toward the final, culminating acts, it will be characterized by strife, war, natural upheavals, and general catastrophes. It is not a pretty picture. But it is a factual one. However, despite such realities, that is not the full picture. Remember our lesson? Things will get a great deal worse *before they get immeasurably better*! In other words, the bad part is not the last part! The last part is the glorious arrival of the King and the establishment of His everlasting kingdom!

When I worked as a chaplain to cancer patients and their families, I noticed that there were patients who did not fear death but who did fear dying. In other words, their identity in Christ was secure. They knew where they would spend eternity. God was the Shepherd who was with them, leading them "through the valley of the shadow of death" (Psalm 23:4). They longed to finally be in His presence. They knew that for them it would only be "a flash . . . the twinkling of an eye" (1 Corinthians 15:52), from breathing their last to standing before Him. So they were not afraid to face death.

What did scare them, however, was dying. Losing control of their decision-making capacities, their bodily functions, their awareness of their surroundings, as well as not knowing how their death would actually occur, and how painful it might be—all of these things *did* elicit fear. The medical and support staff did everything possible to help them through this process.

Facing the future and the Second Coming is similar. Those who belong to Christ *need never fear His coming*! It is indeed good news! However, there likely *should* be a healthy concern, or perhaps even fear, over the events that will transpire before His coming. It will only be through His grace and strength that His children will survive.

A third lesson follows these two. In light of the fact that *what seems lasting really isn't,* and that *it will get a great deal worse before it gets immeasurably better,* it becomes vital for the Christian to have a well-founded understanding of how to *live.* Thus, *watching is not an act but a lifestyle.* And since how we watch is a lifestyle, *when* Jesus comes is simply not as important as *that* He will come.

We should reject, then, the "days of adrenaline" approach to preparing for the coming. No doubt times of excitement will come. The prospect of Christ coming again *should* elicit enthusiasm. However, a method of watching and waiting for the coming that depends considerably on excitement and adrenaline is to be rejected as the *means* of preparing for the Advent.

When I leave my house, I sometimes leave a task for my children to accomplish while I am gone. I am certainly interested in them being obedient and finishing the task by the time of my return. However, I am at least as (if not *more*) interested in them learning to conduct themselves in certain ways during my absence. Therefore, if I know that they waste the time while I am gone only to suddenly spring into action when they realize I am just around the bend, I am disappointed, *even if they are able to finish the task by the time I enter the house.* Why? Because such an approach is based too much on chance, leads to too much laziness, has the wrong motivation, and creates too much risk that they will not learn the kinds of lessons that will serve them well in life. On the other hand, it says much about the maturity of a child who will throw herself into the task at hand regardless of when Mom or Dad might come home. Similarly, there is much to be said for the employee who will do his work, regardless of whether or not the boss is watching.

Could it be that such followers are the kind Jesus wants? Followers who obediently set about the doing of His will, whether they believe He will come tomorrow or at some point well into the future. Followers whose *life* belongs to Him, regardless of whether He comes in their lifetime or not. Followers whose lives exhibit faithfulness to His will, whether they think He is a long way down the road or just around the corner. Such followers will be much more interested in the *lifestyle* that watches than they will be in the *act* of watching.

Do not forget that in Matthew 24 and 25 Jesus does not speak of being ready *then*. No! He speaks of being ready *now*! *Today! Always!* Such reminds us that readiness for the coming is a way we live our lives.

Out of this grows our fourth lesson: *Our focus should be at least as much on the present as it is on the future.* Some Protestants— and evangelicals in particular—have historically so focused on the future that they have expressed little, if any, concern or interest in the present state of the world around us (other than to critique it negatively). However, as life continues and Christ does not appear, there is disappointment and even disillusionment. Then there comes the tendency to swing too far in the other direction, and become *exclusively* focused on the present and forget the eternal future altogether. Thus it is possible to end up swinging back and forth on an unhealthy pendulum between an almost total focus on the future, or an obsession with present life.

One pastor from Florida is said to have described it this way: "It's hard to get my people to think about eternity. In the wintertime it's so beautiful here that that they don't want to think about heaven, and in the summertime it's so hot that hell doesn't scare them!"

For those who believe in the coming of Christ, a natural outgrowth of such belief has sometimes been to ignore or even depreciate the present world. Concern over such things as the political system or the environment have been discouraged After all, is it not true that all these things will be destroyed "by fire, and the elements will melt in the heat" (2 Peter 3:12)? However, the same God who created our bodies as temples of the Holy Spirit (see 1 Corinthians 6:19, 20), also created the earth. Though both are marred by sin, both still bear the fingerprints of the Creator. And the Creator expects us to care for both, and will, in fact, call to task those who destroy either (see, for example, Revelation 11:18). Just as we have only one body, and are expected to care for it, so we have only one earth, and are expected to care for it. Thus, while we live as those who expect "a better country—a heavenly one" (Hebrews 11:16), we still live now as citizens of *this* country, our earthly abode. And as such, we do the best we can to live as faithful citizens. We pay our taxes, respect and support our governments (as far as possible), we vote, participate in efforts to improve our neighborhoods, and take care of our environment. In other words, we are the best citizens our country has (see passages such as Romans 13:1–7 and 1 Peter 2:13–25).

Do we do this because we believe that this world is all we have? Or because we believe that humanity can pull itself up by its bootstraps and create a utopia on this earth? Or because we have put our anticipation of the Second Advent on the back burner and therefore must focus primarily on the here and now? *No!* Positively not. We do it because we seek to be faithful children of the Christ who "richly provides us with everything for our enjoyment" (1 Timothy 6:17), and who—as any parent might—expects us to care for it until He comes for us. We do it because our Lord told us to "occupy [read: *care for*] till I come" (Luke 19:13, KJV). We do it because *He created it* and *He oversees it* and we love Him. And one way to show our love is to do our best in the present to care for what He has given us.

Finally, a lesson we cannot disregard is that *we must maintain a view toward the big picture.* I once read of a church whose members decided that they were going to read the book of Revelation all the way through in an attempt to understand what God wanted to say to them through its images. So they waded into the book with sometimes confusing metaphors and beasts and images. They might have become bogged down by the many details they did not understand. However, they decided to maintain a view toward the big picture. And as they did so, they drew a variety of conclusions such as: Human history will become dramatically dangerous prior to the coming; the lines of demarcation between God's people and His enemies will become increasingly distinct; God will care for His own; and, in the end, God wins!

They were not able to answer all of the questions about the intricacies of Revelation. They did not come to clear conclusions about every image, every beast, and every metaphor. But they did come away from the experience with a profound sense of the ability of God to care for His own, all the way into the kingdom. They saw the big picture, and the big picture provided them with the most critical information and the most vibrant hope.

When all else has been said and done, there is one final take-home lesson. And it is the point not only of the Christian's life, but of these chapters in Matthew, and indeed of all of Christian history. And that lesson is this simple verity: *He will come!*

It seems odd to say that, doesn't it? After all, what surrounds us in our world seems so lasting. It seems that things will go on as they always have. And sure, things are bad; in fact, at times they are terrible. But we always hang on to hope, hang on to the promise that things will get better, hang on to the belief that all things will go on as they always have. But if we believe in the Christ who came, we also believe in the Christ who *will* come. And this is the Christ who, in the midst of these words of His coming, said simply, "Heaven and earth will pass away, but my words will never pass away" (Matthew 24:35).

So, lift up the trumpet and loud let it ring! *Jesus is coming again!*

Dedicatory Prayer

God of the ages, Christ of the coming,
we dedicate ourselves to You. We long for an eternally
bright tomorrow to soon burst upon the stage of human life,
but we are committed to journeying with Jesus
until that day arrives. May Your smile of acceptance,
Your touch of empowerment, and Your caress of grace
rest upon each of us today. Strengthen us in a weak world,
purify us in a wicked world, enlighten us in a dark world
that we may journey with Jesus all the way
into the kingdom of God.
In the name of the Christ of the kingdom,
Amen.

Thought and Discussion Questions

Chapter 1

1. In your formative years, how did you relate to the issue of the second coming of Christ and the end of the world?

2. What is your predominant emotional reaction to that theme now?

3. Have you ever responded to the theme of the Advent in either of the two ways described in this chapter *(relinquishing your beliefs* or *reaffirming our traditional approach)*? If so, are you satisfied with such a response?

4. What do you believe to be a realistic, faith-affirming way to approach the coming of Christ?

Chapter 2

1. Have you thought about the end of time more or less than you did before September 11, 2001?

2. Reflect on stories you have heard over the years which claimed to signal an immediate end. How did they affect you?

3. Are you aware of asking *when?* and *what?* Why or why not?

4. Why do you think Jesus didn't just tell His disciples when the coming would occur?

Chapter 3

1. What signs of Christ's coming do you see around you?

2. How have you related to the repetitive nature of the signs Jesus gives in Matthew 24?

3. How do you interpret Ellen White's quotation in *Testimonies for the Church* (quoted in this chapter), in light of the events of September 11, 2002?

4. Do you agree that the signs Jesus gives are more like highway *identification* signs than they are like highway *distance* signs? Why or why not?

Chapter 4

1. Why do you think Christians in general, and Seventh-day Adventists in particular, have shown such a tendency to try to set a date for the return of Christ?

2. Name some of the different ways you have seen Christians define what it means to watch for the coming of Christ. Which of those are legitimate, biblical ways of watching? Which are not?

3. If the servant in the parable makes the choice not to watch, why would he make that choice? If he makes the choice to watch, why would he make that choice?

4. Do you agree with the idea of the last paragraph of the chapter? Why or why not?

Chapter 5

1. What has happened to your belief in the Second Coming and your faith in Jesus Christ (and the faith of others around you) as the Bridegroom has delayed His coming?

2. Do you agree with the assertion of this chapter that it is possible to be both *wise* and *asleep*? Both *asleep* and *ready*?

3. This chapter makes the statement: "The servant [in the previous parable] was surprised by the arrival of his master. In this parable, the bridesmaids are surprised by the arrival of the groom. But in each case the surprise is not that the master or the groom came *sooner* than was expected. No, the surprise is that the master and the groom returned *later* than was expected. The surprise was the *delay*!" How does this challenge or change the way you think about being surprised by the coming of Christ?

4. In what ways can we nurture an ongoing relationship with Jesus Christ so that it remains vital and vibrant, even though the coming happens later than we expect it to?

Chapter 6

1. This parable is sometimes interpreted as merely saying that we need to use what we have been given. How does placing the parable into its original context of watching for the coming of Christ change or enlarge its meaning?

2. What talents do you have that you can put to use for the enlarging of the kingdom?

3. What does *fear* do to your use of your talents? What scares you about using your talents?

4. If a central part of watching means using your talents to increase God's kingdom, in what ways are you currently watching?

Chapter 7

1. How does knowing the object of your giving change your attitude toward giving?

2. Do you agree with Margaret Mead's assessment on page 96? Why or why not?

3. Where do you think "Jesus" has crossed your path in the last twenty-four hours? How would it have changed your response had that *actually been* Jesus? Suppose your response would have changed had it actually been Jesus—what does that tell you?

4. Does the third surprise of the parable surprise you? Why or why not?

Chapter 8

1. In light of the first lesson (on page 104)—what seems to be lasting, *really isn't*—what might you need to change about the way you live your life?

2. This chapter suggests that, relative to the coming of Christ, knowing the big picture might be more important than nailing down all of the details. Do you agree or disagree? Why?

3. Is saying our focus should be at least as much on the present as it is on the future, (as the fourth lesson teaches), placing too much emphasis on the present? Would it be better to place *less* emphasis on the present?

4. What other take-home lessons would you add to the list in this chapter?

If you enjoyed this book, you'll enjoy these as well:

The Cure for the Last Daze

Karl Haffner. Pastor Karl uses his easy-to-understand commentary and personal applications to clear away the prophetic fog and give common folk a clear view of what the Bible teaches about our soon-coming Lord.

0-8163-1960-X. Paperback.

Last Day Events

Ellen G. White. A compilation of statements about the end of time taken from 65 sources—published books, manuscript collections, and material never before published.

0-8163-1879-4. Hardcover.
0-8163-1901-4. Paperback.

How to Think About the End Times

Marvin Moore. Many are having their faith shaken due to disappointment over failed end-time scenarios. Scenarios based on faulty thinking. *Signs* editor Marvin Moore helps us think through end-time events in ways that are balanced, scriptural, and free from unfounded sensationalism.

0-8163-1835-2. Paperback.

Order from your ABC by calling **1-800-765-6955**, or get online and shop our virtual store at www.AdventistBookCenter.com.

- Read a chapter from your favorite book
- Order online
- Sign up for e-mail notices on new products